FUN *without* VULGARITY

Go forth in haste
With bills and paste
Proclaim to all creation
That men are wise
Who advertise
In this our generation.

'Valuable advice' — The Poster, *April 1900*

FUN *without* VULGARITY

Victorian and Edwardian Popular Entertainment Posters

Catherine Haill

Published in association with the Public Record Office

London: The Stationery Office

Applications for reproduction should be made in writing to:
The Controller of Her Majesty's Stationery Office, St Clements House,
2–16 Colegate, Norwich NR3 1BQ

ISBN 0 11 440263 9

British Library Cataloguing in Publication Data
A CIP catalogue record for this book is available from the British Library

Edited, designed and produced by The Stationery Office

Frontispiece: An elegantly dressed flyposter is shown here pasting up a poster advertising *Macbeth* on vacant but inconveniently low wall space! Engraved illustration by Kenneth M Skeaping from *On the Stage and Off,* Jerome K Jerome, Leadenhall Press, 1891 Photo: PRO

Front cover:
Plate 31, *Woman and Wine* by Dudley Hardy. PRO, COPY 1/150 folio 85
Plate 32, *The French Spy* by Arthur Brooke White. PRO, COPY 1/240 folio 297

Back cover (anticlockwise from left):
Plate 22, *Charley's Aunt* by Chadwick Rymer. PRO, COPY 1/124 folio 540
Plate 78, *Moore and Burgess Minstrels* by Chadwick Rymer. PRO, COPY 1/123 folio 200
Plate 13, *A Runaway Girl* by William ('Will.') True. PRO, COPY 1/152 folio 126
Plate 51, *Humpty Dumpty, or, Harlequin the Lost Princess and the Magic Silver Spoon* by W H Pike.
   PRO, COPY 1/76 folio 348
Plate 71, *Grais' Zebras and Baboons* by Albert Whitfield. PRO, COPY 1/315i folio 38

The Stationery Office

Published by The Stationery Office and available from:

The Publications Centre
(mail, telephone and fax orders only)
PO Box 276, London SW8 5DT
General enquiries 0171 873 0011
Telephone orders 0171 873 9090
Fax orders 0171 873 8200

The Stationery Office Bookshops
49 High Holborn, London WC1V 6HB
(counter service and fax orders only) Fax 0171 831 1326
68–69 Bull Street, Birmingham B4 6AD   0121 236 9696   Fax 0121 236 9699
33 Wine Street, Bristol BS1 2BQ   0117 9264306   Fax 0117 9294515
9–21 Princess Street, Manchester M60 8AS   0161 834 7201   Fax 0161 833 0634
16 Arthur Street, Belfast BT1 4GD   01232 238451   Fax 01232 235401
The Stationery Office Oriel Bookshop
The Friary, Cardiff CF1 4AA   01222 395548   Fax 01222 384347
71 Lothian Road, Edinburgh EH3 9AZ (counter service only)

Customers in Scotland may mail, telephone or fax their orders to:
Scottish Publications Sales
South Gyle Crescent, Edinburgh EH12 9EB   0131 479 3141   Fax 0131 479 3142

The Stationery Office's Accredited Agents
(see Yellow Pages)

and through good booksellers

Printed in the UK for The Stationery Office
Dd 303065 C60 11/96

Contents

Acknowledgements

I am especially grateful to Julia Wigg of the Public Record Office for her assistance during this project. I would also like to thank my editor, Kim Yarwood, for her unfailing patience, persistence and good humour. Thanks are also due to Alison Merry, Terry Bloxham and John Francheschina; to Isobel Sinden of the V&A Picture Library; and to the photographers – Andrew Smart of A C Cooper Ltd, Brian Carter of the Public Record Office, and Mike Larkin and Graham Brandon of the Victoria and Albert Museum. Photographs in the Introduction from the Theatre Museum and the Victoria and Albert Museum are reproduced courtesy of the Trustees of the Victoria and Albert Museum.

Above all, I would like to thank Jonathan and our children, Victoria, Olivia and Alexander, without whose support and understanding I could not have completed this book.

Author and publisher are grateful to the Public Record Office, the Theatre Museum and the Board of Trustees of the V&A for their permission to reproduce artwork.

Abbreviations used in artwork credits

PRO   Public Record Office

TM, V&A   Theatre Museum, V&A

Introduction

'Fun without vulgarity' was the image that the Moore and Burgess Minstrels wanted to promote for their minstrel shows which were popular in the last thirty years of the 19th century. Aware of the charges of immorality levelled against some forms of contemporary entertainment, they printed this phrase on their poster, keen to attract respectable audiences with impunity. Most of the productions and performers represented in this book would have liked their efforts to be seen in that light, although some might justly have been accused of vulgarity. All of their posters were undoubtedly fun.

The late Victorian and the Edwardian establishment was particularly sensitive about charges of impropriety. British theatre gained respectability in the second half of the 19th century as actor-managers, including the Bancrofts, Charles Wyndham and Henry Irving, began to attract fashionable audiences to their theatres. Popular entertainment such as burlesque, pantomime and music hall thrived on leggy ladies and *double entendre* in the 1870s and 1880s, but towards the end of the century even that began to change. Burlesque gave way to musical comedy; pantomimes became increasingly spectacular and more suitable for family audiences and variety took over from music hall. When the first Royal Variety Performance took place at the Palace Theatre in 1912, the great music hall star, 'the incomparable' Marie Lloyd, was absent. Her invitation to take part had stipulated that she must tone down her material, which she staunchly refused to do. Marie Lloyd, with her famous flirtatious wink, had risen to fame on her ambiguous comic songs and *double entendre* patter. By 1912 her inimitable style, which had made her a star, was not considered suitable for the king, despite the fact that he would probably have enjoyed every minute of her act, especially 'her winks and her silences'.

The posters in this book reflect this change in attitude. The high-kicking burlesque stars seen on posters during the 1880s were ousted by sophisticated images of respectable stars of musical comedy in the 1890s. The wasp-waisted principal boys adorning pantomime posters were gradually replaced by more elegant representations by accredited poster artists. Variety posters were perhaps the last bastion of the leggy female but even here respectability was breaking through. The poster artist who depicted 'The Beautiful Mademoiselle Nadji' in tights in his 1904 poster [see plate 70], also showed her demurely wearing her best hat!

The popular Miss Marie Lloyd whose suggestiveness came not so much from her material as from the timing and tone with which she delivered it. From a postcard by J Beagles & Co. TM, V&A, GG3841

In the March 1899 issue of *The Poster* the following 'Answer to Correspondents' was printed in reply to an artist's enquiry about the copyright of his poster designs:

> 'You must make a tracing of the sketch and take it, and the sketch, to Stationers' Hall Court, Ludgate Hill; you will have to fill up a form (1d) and pay a fee of One Shilling, and then your design will be copyrighted. Should the drawing be too elaborate, and the tracing require a long time to do, you can take the original drawing with you and give a full written description as to details, colours, etc. But the safest way is the first one.'

The procedure was simpler if the poster was already printed: a copy of the poster itself was deposited at Stationers' Hall along with the form stating the name and address of the artist and that of the copyright holder. In most cases the printer bought the copyright from the artist, who included its price with that of the design, but occasionally the artist or the person who commissioned the poster managed to retain copyright. *The Poster* also had a word of advice for the concerned artist who enquired about the fee for a poster design:

> 'As regards the price of a design for a poster 20 x 30, it all depends on the merit of the work; you must use your own discretion, from £5 to £10 is a fair price.'

The procedure for registering copyright at Stationers' Hall was carried out under Acts of Parliament in force from 1842 until 1912, but registration was optional so thousands of posters were not registered. It was not a cheap exercise since, in addition to the penny for the form and the shilling for the registration, the certificate of registration cost five shillings. We should be immensely grateful to those that did go to the expense since all the posters in this book survived because of registration. Some firms waited quite a while after the poster was in use before they brought a batch of posters to Stationers' Hall for registration. Once registered, posters were folded up and boxed at Stationers' Hall along with their forms, and thus protected from the fatal damage caused to their fellows pasted up on hoardings in the street.

Registration in this way stopped in April 1912. Copyright could be registered after that, but details were simply noted in a register, and it was no longer necessary to deposit a sketch or an example of the finished work. All the posters in this book, registered between November 1885 and March 1912, are now in the extensive archives of Victorian and Edwardian advertising material held in the Public Record Office at Kew. Some were designed for specific productions, some for the performers themselves to promote their acts, and others as stock posters. Various types of stock posters were commissioned and produced by printing firms, with images chosen to fit in with any 'gorgeous pantomime' or 'thrilling melodrama', which could then be overprinted with specific details. In 1900, David Allen & Sons boasted over seven hundred stock posters, promising: 'Such a wide range and variety of subjects is available that pictorials for almost any piece are practically certain to be found among our stock.'

Because registration was optional, the posters reproduced here are not a comprehensive survey of the work of the poster artists of the day, nor of all the types of popular entertainment. Instead, they are a cross-section of good and bad poster design, advertising a wide variety of popular entertainment on offer during those twenty-three years – from melodrama to magic, from pantomime to 'posturers'. Often they give us a faithful view of what the costumes and sets looked like on stage. At a time when photographs inside theatres were a rarity, a poster artist would depict a scene from a show precisely, especially if working on a tour poster, when he could sketch the finished London production for the provincial hoardings, as for *The Dandy Fifth* poster [see plate 14].

The need to register posters in the last two decades of the 19th century stemmed from the increasingly prolific production of colour lithograph posters. As well as entertainment, they advertised travel, seaside resorts, and every sort of product that manufacturers wanted consumers to buy. Advances in printing techniques made large, colourful posters cheaper to produce, and theatre proprietors began to find that the outlay on them was money well spent. By the 1880s, some people began to realise that posters could also have artistic value; in 1881, *The Magazine of Art* published an article entitled 'The Street as Art Galleries', which discussed a poster by Hubert von Herkomer, RA. The idea of an artistic poster nevertheless seemed risible to the author of an article in *Punch* (30 April 1881) who ridiculed the idea of artists being allowed 'the run of advertising hoardings in the Metropolis'. He wondered how the Royal Academician Sir Frederic Leighton would advertise Pears Soap with the classical subject 'Olympus' on a thirty-foot poster hoarding, or how Burne-Jones could adapt one of his damsels to the advertisement of a patent medicine. The writer even ironically suggested that 'culture will become universal, and a mere ride outside a twopenny omnibus, even without a catalogue, will, in itself, afford an artistic treat of the very highest order'. Attitudes changed despite such scepticism, and in 1898, *The Poster* magazine was launched with articles based on interviews with poster artists, criticism of artistic qualities of posters and notes on the latest developments on the hoardings. In June 1900, Charles Hiatt wrote an article in *The Poster* in which he decided that 'the poster is analogous to a fresco painter for external decoration', and advised that a successful poster should combine correct draughtsmanship and fine colour, and that the poster artist 'has just as much need to mix his colours with brains as had Sir Joshua Reynolds himself'.

This depicts the crush that could occur for out-of-town performances by London 'stars', in this case Edmund Kean whose appearance as Othello is advertised on a letterpress poster on the wall. 'Gallery Folks' woodcut by Theodore Lane from Pierce Egan's The Life of an Actor *(M Arnold, 1831). TM, V&A, JA1205*

Entertainment has always needed advertisement. The earliest theatricals were advertised by word of mouth or by hand-written bills. The earliest printed advertisements were typographic, simply printed in black lettering produced by the letterpress process. They served both as advance notice and programme, and gave basic information about the entertainment on offer – the titles of the plays, the times of the performances, the availability of tickets and the names of the best-known performers. Printed daily, they measured approximately 20 cm high by 15 cm wide. They were pasted up outside places of entertainment, given out to passers-by, posted through doors or scattered in the coaches of the gentry. Even as late as the 1860s, small advertisements like this were thrust into the hands of passengers in their hansom cabs (as we learn in Wilkie Collins's novel *No Name*, when the actress's manager wants to advertise her performances). In the 18th century, a few larger printed advertisements – or 'great billes' – were produced by more enterprising and wealthy theatre proprietors, who even introduced red lettering in accord with the French custom. The red-lettered bills proved more attractive than the black ones, as noted in a prologue to a play at the Haymarket Theatre in 1706, which advised:

'Put out Red-letter'd Bills, and raise your Price
You'll lure a select Audience in a trice.'

However, red lettering was more expensive than black, and Drury Lane expense vouchers for 1712–16 show that red bills cost fifteen shillings daily, as opposed to ten shillings for black. 'Great Billes', the immediate ancestor of the theatre poster, were costly too – in the 18th century, all paper was hand-made, and larger advertisements represented a greater outlay on publicity.

Engravers clearly relished circus subjects, and the resulting attendance figures would have justified the extra expense of the novel publicity. Detailed wood engravings advertise this performance by Mr Carter, the popular 'Lion King', at Astley's Circus, 26 August 1844.
TM, V&A, S.1790

Circus proprietors led the way for pictorial posters advertising entertainment. When circus began in Britain, in the late 18th century, it presented a tremendous number of exciting moments ripe for illustration to attract potential audiences: a man could turn somersaults from horseback; a trainer of wild animals could soothe lions and tigers in their cage. The early development of circus coincided with the invention in England, in 1801, of the first machine that could manufacture paper in a continuous sheet. Paper costs dropped dramatically, and circuses began to print long playbills to which they added woodcut illustrations to whet the appetites of passers-by for the thrills of the ring. This was especially helpful for the many illiterate people, who could not make sense of a jumble of letters but who naturally understood a picture. An added bonus for the circus proprietor was that illiterate bill stickers would no longer post the bills upside-down! Exhibitors of exotic animals and 'curiosities' also appreciated the advantages of showing a picture of the wondrous sights on offer for their patrons on their handbills.

Where popular entertainment led in the early 19th century, proprietors of the so-called 'patent theatres' were slow to follow, perhaps because they looked upon popular entertainment and their gaudy coloured playbills with disdain. There was an historical reason for this superciliousness. From the 1660s until 1843 there was a division in Britain between those theatres which could offer plays featuring only the spoken word and those whose entertainments had to include music and dancing. This situation originated from two patents that Charles II had issued to permit Killigrew's Men and Davenant's Men to perform drama after the Restoration, and was reinforced in 1737 by the Licensing Act, which forbade the production of plays which consisted only of speech in unlicensed theatres. This originally worked in the favour of the 'patent theatres', protecting their position and preventing others producing drama. The proprietors of Covent Garden and Drury Lane Theatres enjoyed the exclusive right to call themselves 'Theatres Royal' until after 1750, when royal patents were also issued to a number of provincial theatres.

By the 1830s the situation was unworkable. Other London theatres had been granted the right to present plays during the summer break which was taken by the 'patent houses'; there was a huge increase in the building of unlicensed places of entertainment, and the theatres which were not permitted to perform the 'straight drama' repertoire of the patent houses did so anyway, simply including five songs per act to circumvent the regulations! In any case, the programmes on offer at the 'minor' theatres were so popular that the proprietors of the patent theatres at Covent Garden and Drury Lane began to produce identical entertainment.

The patent theatres' monopoly of so-called 'legitimate' drama became unworkable, and in 1843 the Theatre Regulation Act abolished the legal basis of the patent theatres. Nevertheless, after 1843 it was still largely the producers of popular entertainment who adorned their playbills with exciting images. In the 1850s, the earnest actor-manager Charles Kean increased the size of his playbills in order to accommodate lengthy descriptions in black lettering on white paper, detailing the scenery in his productions and the authorities he had consulted to ensure the accuracy of his stage settings. At the same time, playbills for melodrama, magic, pantomime, circus, and pleasure gardens gave the public multi-coloured posters with a variety of ornamental letter-forms and woodcut, engraved or lithographic images advertising the entertainment that they relished.

Melodrama plots crowded with incident inspired the illustration of letterpress posters. Woodcut engravings on this advertisement for Jack Sheppard *at the Theatre Royal, Adelphi, 2 December 1839, depict highlights of the action. TM, V&A, FF708*

In the 18th century, all typographic printing was done by hand on wooden presses. After 1800, iron presses took over, followed by steam-powered cylinder presses – the invention of a German engineer, Friedrich König. By 1820, there were eight powered printing presses in London, mainly used by the newspaper industry. They were expensive to install and complicated for old-fashioned printers to use. New, powered letterpress presses were developed, but as late as 1850, mechanised presses were still regarded as something of a novelty, with printers noting with pride on their posters the fact that they were 'steam printers'.

All of these methods were used for typeface only: images on a poster still had to be added separately. Lithography had been developed as a method of reproducing images as early as 1798, by a German playwright called Aloys Senefelder. He discovered that the porous surface of limestone could absorb marks from a waxy crayon which, in turn, retained printer's ink when unmarked areas were cleaned with a mixture of turpentine and water. By preparing sets of stones, each inked in a different colour, careful overprinting could even produce coloured images without the need for hand-colouring. Artists began to experiment with this technique, but lithographic stones were heavy to use manually. In 1851, an Austrian engineer, Georg Siegl, took out patents in Austria and France for a powered machine which could print from lithographic stones, incorporating rollers which damped and inked them automatically. Zinc plates were soon developed to replace the heavy lithographic limestones, and by the middle of the century, lithography was a commercial proposition.

Theatre managers began to realise that they could now advertise their productions with far subtler images than had been seen before. They also saw that detailed information about cast lists was superfluous in a pictorial advertisement: from the late 1850s, some theatres began to issue programmes that gave their patrons that sort of information when they reached the theatre. As theatres gradually moved from changing their programmes nightly to producing 'runs' of plays, so the production of both programmes and posters became more viable.

In an article entitled 'Posters and Poster Printing', printed in the theatrical magazine *The Era* (December 1883), the author reported on new paper-cutting machines and the way that some could print in eight or ten colours in one process, a remarkable technical advance. He gave details of a particular machine which was fitted with a 'taking off' device, patented by Messrs Swan and Co., which paid for itself in fifteen months, thanks to the saving in boys' wages. Visiting Messrs Stannard & Sons, the printers demonstrated 'zincography' to him, a process which was also used for posters. It was cheaper than lithography – two thousand impressions could be taken from one plate – but the results were less subtle. Nevertheless, they were good enough for huge advertisements made up of many separate sheets, pasted together like a jigsaw puzzle. Stannard & Sons had branched out into theatre poster manufacture by the 1880s, but the firm had begun in the 1840s, under the name William Stannard, and was already famous for its lithographed music sheet covers. Thousands of the music cover lithographic stones were stored in Stannard's office, lining the shelves from ceiling to floor, like books on bookshelves. This was possible with the smaller stones used for music titles, but storage of a large number of lithographic stones for posters must have been difficult!

The earliest colour lithograph posters from the 1860s were small, but they gradually increased in size, and by 1900, huge advertisements were appearing on the streets, comprising many sheets. A poster for the tour of the Adelphi Theatre's *Harbour Lights* (1899) was made up of fifty-six double crown posters, printed in twenty-eight parts and five colours. One hundred and forty stones were needed: one for each colour, twenty-eight times. Each stone cost about £5 and weighed nearly seven hundredweight. The poster cost £600 per thousand to produce, on top of which was the additional expense of three pence a sheet for the bill poster.

This meant that every time the poster was displayed, it cost fourteen shillings and, since fifty copies might be needed for a town such as Manchester or Birmingham, that meant an outlay of £35 per town, or almost £2,000 for the whole tour – a huge sum in those days. Such costs were not unusual, though, and George Alexander's accounts from St James's Theatre show that in 1900 he spent £1,340 15s 2d on 'advertising and bill-posting' for his production *The Man of Forty*. It was obviously worth it, since the production ran for one hundred and twenty performances and made a profit.

With the technical advances in poster production came new problems concerning the poster hoardings, and even the bill stickers themselves. In his essay 'Bill-Sticking' (*Household Words*, March 1851), Charles Dickens interviewed 'The King of the Bill Stickers', who recalled that in the 1780s, when posters were small, women were employed to paste up the bills, using a piece of wood called a 'dabber' for the job. Men took over as posters became larger, and an attempt was made to start bill-sticking firms, but fights over poster sites frequently broke out between stickers. No poster was safe from having a rival poster pasted on top, or even from the process of 'black-washing' – painting over your rivals' posters. Recalling a fight in Trafalgar Square, the Poster King concluded: 'A bill sticker ought to be able to handle his fists a bit.'

According to the Poster King, auctioneers paid bill stickers working in towns five shillings a day including the cost of paste, whilst men who paraded sandwich boards got £1 a week. If bill stickers could not find effective illegal sites for their posters, they were forced to pay for the privilege:

'We then took possession of the hoarding in Trafalgar Square; but Messrs Grissel and Peto would not allow us to post our bills on the said hoarding without paying them two hundred and fifty pounds for that hoarding, and likewise the hoarding of the Reform Club-house, Pall Mall.'

Renting out hoarding sites became profitable – as it is today – and in 1899 *The Poster* magazine observed that a poster hoarding in 'a good thoroughfare' would cost £200–£300 a year to rent, and that a hoarding near a London railway station had been hired for £1,500! The going rate for renting a hoarding beside a railway line was £10–£30 a year. The sides of horse-drawn carriages were also used as authorised locations for bills: an article in *The Poster* credited the advertising manager of the Palace Theatre as being the first manager to use 'an artistic 'bus bill' in place of the previous typographic ones.

By the turn of the century, the organised bill-posting trade had formed the Billposters' Protection Association to safeguard their rights and influence public bodies when necessary. In 1890 they set up a Joint Censorship Committee to enable them to protect the public from shocking or indecent images on posters. By 1900, the association had six hundred members, their own magazine and their own publication, *The Bill Poster*, issued from 1886 to 1920, 'to repel attacks and promote the prosperity of the trade'. The association negotiated issues close to their

This poster sticker outside London's Surrey Theatre has a pot of glue conveniently strapped to his waist. Since he is shown without a ladder, the poster was probably initially attached to the wall by means of the dabber with which he is working. Detail of 'A View of Surrey Theatre'; etching published by Robert Laurie and James Whittle.
TM, V&A, BW41826

THE KNIFEBOARD OF AN OMNIBUS.

LEYBOURNE

GEORGE LEYBOURNE
STACEY LEE ESQ.   R. COOTE.

Public transport has long been a vehicle for advertising. The artist Alfred Concanen incorporates an advertisement for an appearance by the music hall star George Leybourne in this music sheet cover: The Knifeboard of an Omnibus, as sung by Leybourne. Colour lithograph printed by Concanen Siebe & Co., c.1880.
TM, V&A, BW41824

members' interests, such as the proposal by the London County Council to reduce the size of hoardings on vacant land to ten feet. Following the Association's intervention, the limit was increased to twelve feet and since by this time the bill-posting firms employed a large number of the former 'flyposters', they considered that there was less illegal bill-posting than hitherto.

The wages earned by bill stickers hardly increased much since Dickens wrote about wages in 1851; in May 1901 an advertisement in *The Era* stated:

'Wanted, Bill-Poster. Good steady man. Wages 26/- a week and house, coal and gas free. Must send references. 107 Derby Road, Bootle, Liverpool.'

By the 1880s and 1890s, popular entertainment at home and abroad inspired the most colourful and

A grand name did not ensure a grand poster. Here a sandwich board man advertises Adelina Patti's appearance at Covent Garden 'tonight' with a plain typographic poster. 'The London Season: Kensington Gardens'; engraving reproduced in The Illustrated London News, *1895. PRO, ZPER 34/106*

lavish posters. In France, the superb colour lithograph posters of Toulouse-Lautrec and Chéret featured circus, dance and cabaret performers; in England, it became increasingly important for variety performers to have pictorial posters to advertise their acts, but more serious forms of theatre clung to typographic posters. In 1895, the aerial performer Graceful Gertrella had her extravagant poster registered [see plate 67], while in the same year an engraving from *The Illustrated London News* shows a sandwich board man parading in Kensington Gardens with a basic typographic poster advertising the return of the great opera singer Adelina Patti to Covent Garden. It is fitting, therefore, that the first ever British exhibition of posters took place in November 1894 at London's Royal Aquarium in Toothill Street, Westminster. This was built in 1875 with an arched glass roof similar to that of the Crystal Palace, and became famous for its huge, 600-gallon water tank in the basement where swimming exhibitions took place. Variety performances were the mainstay of the Aquarium, including shows of superhuman strength by the strong men Sandow and Sampson, feats of daring by Zazel, who was shot from a cannon, and the exhibition of 'living wonders'.

Discussing the poster exhibition, the critic in *The Sketch* (November 1894) noted that it was hard at times to concentrate on the posters when the music and noise of the daily show in the arena below was competing for attention:

'Indeed, at moments, even the most ardent devotees of the "fierce placard" were tempted to gaze of the acrobats, *danseuses*, and grotesques, who seemed, in the glamour of the limelight, to have leaped from the walls to take part in the show. At times a group of solemnly-occupied art critics would find a rope-dancer in tights brushing past them, or a learned analysis of decorative art would be cut short by the report of a cannon close by.'

He also emphasised the novelty of a poster exhibition, noting:

'To the uninitiated, all this interest in the poster must seem inexplicable; yet people now not merely observe posters, but collect them.'

Poster collecting was certainly becoming increasingly popular, and in 1893, an article by Charles Hiatt had appeared in the first volume of the magazine *The Studio*, entitled 'The Collecting of Posters: A New Field for Connoisseurs', so perhaps it was not surprising that the first exhibition of posters occurred the following year, having received official sanction from an art magazine.

There were two hundred exhibits in the Westminster Aquarium Poster Exhibition, each listed in the illustrated catalogue prefaced by an essay by Mr J T Clarke. Posters by French artists predominated, with fifty exhibits by Jules Chéret, who had studied colour lithography in London in the 1860s and had set up a workshop in Paris in 1866, specialising in 'artistic posters in colour lithography'. The exhibition also featured several posters by 'Lautrec, the incomparable'. English posters included Frederick Walker's wood-engraved

Frederick Walker's woodcut image of the enigmatic heroine fills the poster for the stage adaptation of Wilkie Collins's novel The Woman in White *at the Olympic Theatre, 9 October 1871. The new dominance of the artwork was noted by contemporary art critics. V&A, 55791*

poster for the 1871 Olympic Theatre adaptation of Wilkie Collins's novel *The Woman in White*. This poster is generally credited as Britain's first successful theatre poster because of its bold design and the predominance of the image (earlier illustrated playbills had generally subordinated the image to the text). Walker himself saw his efforts in designing posters as important, writing in one of his letters, 'I am impressed on doing all I can with a first attempt at what I consider an important branch of art', while the reviewer of the Aquarium Poster Exhibition also acknowledged Walker's contribution, writing:

'The place of honour is rightly awarded to Frederick Walker's *The Woman in White*, probably the first example of any English artist of eminence troubling himself with the matter.'

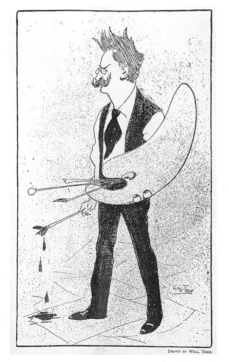

The Poster *magazine featured caricatures of poster artists by fellow artists. This one of Dudley Hardy, his brushes dripping with paint, was by Will. True. Posterdom Caricatures, no. II; from* The Poster *magazine, October 1898. V&A, CT41697*

There were also posters by Aubrey Beardsley and Dudley Hardy, and four by the artists James Pryde and William Nicholson, who became known as 'the Beggarstaff Brothers'.

The influence of Chéret's poster art on Dudley Hardy's style can be witnessed in this book, in his posters for *Woman and Wine* [plate 31] and for *Skipped by the Light of the Moon* [plate 12]. Hardy's posters seems to have been more readily appreciated by theatrical entrepreneurs than the sparse silhouette style of the Beggarstaffs'. In May 1895, their design for a huge advertisement for Henry Irving's production of *Don Quixote* was bought by Irving, but it never appeared on the hoardings. It featured an image of Don Quixote on horseback – the horse seen only in outline against the silhouette of a windmill – but when the actress Ellen Terry later suggested to Irving that the Beggarstaffs should produce a poster for his

Lyceum Theatre production of *Robespierre*, Irving apparently shook his head and declared 'no more mills'. The Beggarstaffs' poster for *Cinderella*, commissioned by the poster firm The Artistic Supply Company for the 1895–96 Drury Lane pantomime, was ridiculed by the star, Dan Leno, who said it looked as if somebody had spilt a pot of paint down it! The proprietor, Augustus Harris, only accepted the poster after the artist, Phil May, congratulated him on having such excellent taste and choosing a brilliant design.

Despite Frederick Walker's innovation, poster art in England acknowledged French influence. The Beggarstaffs admitted a debt to the posters of Toulouse-Lautrec, whom they called 'one of the few artists who understands what a poster is and should be'. Lautrec's distinctive style was influenced by the restraint of Japanese woodcut prints: their predilection for flat blocks of colour, simple silhouettes and unusual viewpoints. In their strength and simplicity, Lautrec's posters were very different from the more frothy and exuberant posters of Jules Chéret. James Pryde and William Nicholson both studied art at Julien's Atelier in Paris, where they saw the 'new' posters adorning the hoardings. As Charles Hiatt wrote in *The Poster* (February 1899):

> 'During their stay in Paris they had the opportunity of seeing all that was being done in the metropolis of artistic announcement. They succumbed neither to the gay blandishments of Chéret nor to the imposing and learned compositions of Grasset. Their attention was probably attracted and retained by the poignant and mordant placards of Toulouse-Lautrec. That they were wisely guided by their instinct can hardly be questioned, for the hoardings have never been adorned with illustrated posters more astonishingly original, more triumphant in their power to attract the attention of the passer-by..'

The majority of posters in this book would not have earned their artists a place in the Aquarium Poster Exhibition of 1894, but they would have attracted the passer-by, achieving the same end, if not by the same means. The 'blood-stained melodramatic style of posters' was as far from the design of posters by Toulouse-Lautrec as Mademoiselle Nadji was from Adelina Patti. The posters that showed several scenes from thrilling melodramas were direct descendants of the earlier posters which were illustrated with small engravings or woodcuts showing exciting highlights of the action. John Stewart Browne – the artist of *Erminie* [plate 1], *Faust Up To Date* [plate 3], *The Solicitor* [plate 21] and *Sherlock Holmes* [plate 33] – told *The Poster* in April 1899 how his poster style had developed from the early days, when lithograph posters succeeded woodcut ones:

> 'In those days an artist could not choose his subjects, and for theatrical posters, a full stage, crammed, jammed full of figures, was the fashion. Any piece of background left blank was a fearful crime, an evidence of scamped work.'

He said that poster designers knew much better by 1899, thanks to the French, but added that the earliest lithographs had all the qualities of the modern ones – black outline and flat colour – and yet the facility for fine shading offered by colour lithographs 'was responsible for the stippled and ineffective style, which has been immediately killed by the new flat one, posted beside it'. Browne complained that it was hard to get advertisers to embrace new styles since they preferred stereotyped posters to something modern. This is apparent in the persistent appearance of the 'jammed full' style of melodrama poster in the 1890s. Old preferences die hard, and whenever a poster like this was wanted, Stafford & Co. could always commission their prolific artist, Thomas Phillips, designer of *Babes in the Wood*, *Robinson Crusoe* and *Vetah* [plates 45, 47 and 2], all 1886, and *Never Despair*, *Sanger's Grand Circus* and *Shadows of a Great City* [plates 26, 54 and 28], all registered in 1887.

There were many poster artists who could turn out work like Phillips, but Dudley Hardy's posters have a style and a feeling for decorative poster art that few artists have achieved since. He trained as a painter and illustrator, and had his first painting hung at the Royal Academy in 1885, when he was only eighteen. Nevertheless, his lasting fame is due to his work commissioned by Waterlow & Sons for the 'galleries of the street' – the poster hoardings. His posters for Augustus Harris's 1894 production of *The Gaiety Girl* were so striking that during its run at the Gaiety Theatre, a frieze of them was pasted round the outside of the theatre. As soon as his poster advertising the magazine *Today* appeared on the hoardings, Hardy's reputation was secure. In 1898, *The Poster* remarked on his originality, his variety of style and the 'refined sauciness' of his work, printing a picture of *Tommy Dodd* [plate 24] and singling out *Cinderella* [plate 50] for special praise:

> 'Cinderella, a tall, graceful figure in white, with hair to match, is walking up a red staircase, past a row of bowing flunkeys, whose head and shoulders only are shown. The walls are green, and the effect of the colour in conjunction with the graceful figure of Cinderella, was graceful in the extreme. This poster was reproduced in several sizes, all of which, and especially the largest, have a distinct market value.'

John Hassall was another outstanding turn-of-the-century poster artist, represented in this book by his posters for *The D'Oyly Carte Opera Company* [plate 17], and *Amasis* [plate 18]. Hassall was an almost exact contemporary of Hardy, and like him, studied art abroad. He turned to poster art later. Hassall's first poster, for the musical comedy *The French Maid*, was produced in 1894 after he responded to a circular letter sent to artists from the printing firm David Allen & Sons, asking if they could produce 'designs for commercial placards'. He did a lot of successful work for the theatre, but perhaps his best-known poster was *Skegness Is So Bracing*, advertising the joys of the seaside resort. In an article in *The Poster* (June 1900), the author credited the Beggarstaffs, Dudley Hardy and John Hassall as the 'three' most representative and contemporary influential poster artists, crediting Aubrey Beardsley, too, 'who removed from English poster designing the charge of lack of originality. What Beardsley began, the Beggarstaffs completed.' The writer decided:

> 'The Beggarstaffs invented a formula; Mr Dudley Hardy found one ready to hand, and proceeded joyfully to experiment in it; Mr Hassall has, so to speak,

Will. True's caricature of the poster artist John Hassall makes a feature of his sinuously curling cigarette smoke. Posterdom Caricatures, no. VI; from The Poster *magazine, March 1899. V&A, CT41698*

PLATE 1

Erminie

*Birmingham Grand Theatre,
26 October 1885
Comedy Theatre,
9 November 1885*

*By Claxson Bellamy
and Harry Paulton
Music by Edward Jakobowski*

The two villains posturing on this poster for the comic opera *Erminie* are Ravennes, played by the tall and wiry Frank Wyatt, and his diminutive sidekick, Cadeau, played by Harry Paulton. The plot revolves around their robbing Erminie's fiancé and their subsequent impersonation of a marquis and a baron at a ball in a château. Their 'Thieves' Duet' and their 'Thieves' cancan' were both popular features of the production, which starred Florence St John in the title role.

Erminie was tried out in Birmingham and Brighton before coming to London, where it was well-received, even Erminie's dreadfully maudlin lullaby – 'Dear mother, in dreams I see thee' – which she sang in the ballroom scene. By December, Marie Tempest took over the title role, and it ran at the Comedy Theatre well into 1886, when a second touring company was formed by Violet Melnotte to take it to the provinces.

Miss Melnotte, the lessee of the Comedy Theatre and director of *Erminie*, appeared in the opera. She was the wife of Frank Wyatt, and when, in 1892, she and Wyatt had the Duke of York's Theatre built in St Martin's Lane, then a slum area, she earned the nickname 'Mad Melnotte'.

PRO reference: COPY 1/73
folio 336
Artist: John Stewart Browne
Printer: Clement-Smith & Co.
Registered: February 1889

Burlesque, Comic Opera and Musical Comedy

Burlesque, Comic Opera and Musical Comedy

PLATE 2

Vetah

*Theatre Royal,
Portsmouth,
30 August 1886*

*Libretto by
Kate Santley
Music by
Kate Santley
and Jacobi*

Comic opera fever was at its zenith in 1886, the year after *The Mikado*'s success. Kate Santley had appeared in music hall, pantomime, comic opera and burlesque, and was a regular performer at the Alhambra Theatre in the 1870s, as well as manager of the Royalty Theatre, 1877–1879. When she tried her hand at writing a comic opera, the oriental splendour of the settings and costumes received more acclaim than the opera itself.

Kate is seen here as Vetah, daughter of an English officer who becomes a favourite at the Rajah's court, narrowly escaping marriage to him before being united with his long-lost nephew, Prince Nafnez.

'A new and original Indian comic opera', *Vetah* toured other provincial towns, but was never produced in London.

PRO reference: COPY 1/76 folio 247
Artist: Thomas Phillips
Printer: Stafford & Co.
Registered: October 1886

PLATE 3
Faust Up To Date

Gaiety Theatre,
30 October 1888

By Henry Pettitt and
George R Sims
Music by Meyer Lutz

A glimpse of stocking may have been shocking in 1888, but it was certainly part of the attraction of Gaiety Theatre burlesques, as was the 'Pas de Quatre' dance which the four girls are seen here spiritedly performing. Meyer Lutz's tune for this dance in *Faust Up To Date* soon became a popular melody and the Gaiety Theatre signature tune.

Gounod's *Faust* provided an excellent target for Pettit and Sims's humour, despite many earlier burlesques of it and the spectacular dramatic version which Henry Irving mounted at London's Lyceum Theatre in 1885. In the Gaiety version, Faust falls in love with Marguerite after seeing her at the Italian Exhibition in Nuremberg, where she was a barmaid.

As usual in burlesques, the text was peppered with excruciating puns and topical references, as when Valentine is saved from the point of Mephistopheles's sword by his Waterbury watch. The title, *Faust Up To Date*, emphasised the contemporary aspects of the piece, and with the popular Florence St John starring as Marguerite, it ran for 180 performances in London before going on tour.

PRO reference: COPY 1/112
folio 82
Artist: John Stewart Browne
Printer: David Allen & Sons Ltd
Registered: March 1894

Burlesque, Comic Opera and Musical Comedy

PLATE 4

Carmen Up To Data

Liverpool Shakespeare Theatre,
22 September 1890
Gaiety Theatre,
4 October 1890

By Henry Pettitt and
George R Sims
Music by Meyer Lutz

Bizet's opera *Carmen* had been popular in London since its first performance at Her Majesty's Theatre in 1878. With its Spanish setting and exotic characters, it was a perfect subject for a Gaiety burlesque, written by the authors and composer of *Faust Up To Data*. Percy Anderson, the costume designer for several Gilbert and Sullivan operas, dressed the Gaiety chorus girls as Spanish ladies and toreadors. Reviewers agreed that the chorus had never looked more alluring.

Florence St John, seen here as Carmen, was born in Devon and ran away from home at the age of fourteen to become a performer. Her first appearance in London was at the Oxford Music Hall in 1878, singing ballads. By 1885, when she starred in *Erminie* [see plate 1] she was already an established favourite, dubbed 'the Queen of Comic Opera' and 'the Queen of Burlesque'. In 1888, she played Marguerite in the Gaiety Theatre's *Faust Up To Date* [see plate 3].

Excellent publicity was also a feature of this production, for which more than one poster was issued. Letty Lind played Mercedes in *Carmen Up To Data* and was depicted on a separate poster [see plate 5].

PRO reference: COPY 1/93
folio 110
Artist: Augusta Lizzie Beecher
Printer: The National Litho
& Printing Co. Ltd
Registered: November 1890

Burlesque, Comic Opera and Musical Comedy

PLATE 5

Carmen Up To Data

*Liverpool Shakespeare Theatre,
22 September 1890
Gaiety Theatre,
4 October 1890*

*By Henry Pettitt and
George R Sims
Music by Meyer Lutz*

Letty Lind is featured here as Mercedes in *Carmen Up To Data*, in the companion poster to that featuring Florence St John in the title role [see plate 4]. Letty Lind joined the Gaiety company in 1887 at the age of twenty-five, to dance in George Edwardes' first Gaiety burlesque, *Monte Christo Jnr*. A Birmingham girl, Lind first appeared on stage, aged five, in *Uncle Tom's Cabin* at the Theatre Royal, Birmingham. At six, she appeared in London as Cinderella in Hengler's Circus, and she subsequently worked regularly as the child performer 'La Petite Letitia'. She became a great favourite as a dancer, especially with her 'skirt dancing', when she twirled a concertina-pleated skirt to great effect.

Letty Lind was regarded as one of the most engaging performers in burlesque. Her child-like charm and stage presence enchanted audiences, and despite her lack of singing voice, she sang a song in *Carmen Up To Data* featuring farmyard imitations. After her career at the Gaiety, she became a favourite at Daly's, with more animal songs.

Carmen Up To Data was such a success that George Edwardes regularly presented 'new editions' of it, and it ran at the Gaiety Theatre for 248 performances.

PRO reference: COPY 1/93
folio 111
Artist: Augusta Lizzie Beecher
Printer: The National Litho & Printing Co. Ltd
Registered: November 1890

Burlesque, Comic Opera and Musical Comedy

JOAN of ARC

OPERA COMIQUE

THE NATIONAL LITHO & PRING C.º A H CHAMBERLYN 115 STRND

Burlesque, Comic Opera and Musical Comedy

PLATE 6

Joan of Arc

*Opera Comique,
17 January 1891
Transferred to Gaiety Theatre,
30 September 1891
Transferred to Shaftesbury
Theatre, 21 December 1891*

*By J L Shine and Adrian Ross
Music by F Osmond Carr*

The story of Joan of Arc does not today seem a likely subject for burlesque, but in the best tradition of the Opera Comique, George Edwardes presented a nonsensical piece whose characters included the unlikely-sounding Bishop of Bovril as well as the New York Herald.

The sombre depiction of Joan on the poster, as played by Marion Hood, also featured on the Opera Comique programme but, despite this, the story revolved around the Constable of France, as played by Arthur Roberts. Roberts was a music hall star and a stalwart of burlesques and musical comedy. His big number in this – 'I'm a regular Randy Pandy O!' – satirised Lord Randolph Churchill (father of Winston) who had just been the centre of a parliamentary storm and had left the government for Africa, as a correspondent for *The Daily Graphic* and to shoot game. Roberts's song, performed in pseudo-colonial garb, mocked Lord Randolph's greed. Churchill soon saw to it that the Censor's blue pencil expunged the song from later performances.

PRO reference: COPY 1/93
folio 109
Artist: Augusta Lizzie Beecher
Printer: The National Litho &
Printing Co. Ltd
Registered: January 1891

PLATE 7

The Lady Slavey

Northampton Opera House,
4 September 1893
Avenue Theatre,
20 October 1894

By George Dance
Music by John Crook

This style of this tour poster for *The Lady Slavey* is reminiscent of posters for melodrama which aimed to whet the appetite of potential play-goers by featuring as many incidents as possible from the action.

Dubbed satirically by one reviewer as 'Cinderella-Up-To-Date' (the Gaiety Theatre had produced the popular burlesque *Cinder-Ellen Up-Too-Late* in 1891), this musical comedy was a tale of mistaken identity and the triumph of love, and was also based loosely on the Cinderella story. The cartwheeling figure in the centre of the poster is the heroine – Phyllis – who dresses as her father's parlourmaid to lend him a status he cannot afford. Her two attractive sisters compete with her for the attentions of the 'Tomato King', an American millionaire. For complicated reasons, he is impersonated by the bailiff, seen here in exaggerated American dress, smoking a cigar and firing a revolver in the air.

George Dance, author of *The Lady Slavey*, was familiar with the ingredients of a good musical comedy since his main occupation was as a provincial tour organiser for London's most popular ones.

PRO reference: COPY 1/117
folio 98
Artist: Charles Frederick Noble
Printer: David Allen & Sons Ltd
Registered: May 1899

PLATE 8

The Bric-a-Brac Will

Lyric Theatre, 28 October 1895

Libretto by S J Adair Fitzgerald and Hugh Moss
Lyrics by S J Adair Fitzgerald
Music by Emilio Pizzi

The picturesque setting of Venice, a huge success in Gilbert and Sullivan's *The Gondoliers* (1889), was also the backdrop for *The Bric-a-Brac Will*, a comic opera about a Venetian duke forced by the terms of a will to marry the lady who owned a certain vase or item of 'bric-à-brac'.

The poster artist crams his poster with moments from the action. He depicts the Duke in a gondola with his preferred bride, Sylvia; the Plaza scene, when all the girls in Venice claim his hand because they each own a forged pot; the poor potter identifying the genuine vase, and the Act II chorus dancing round a camp fire 'in gauzy attire'.

This production ran for over three months at the Lyric Theatre, despite receiving dreadful reviews. One critic did not mince his words, calling it 'excessively feeble and not in the least funny', condemning its 'rambling, inconsequent and purposeless libretto'. He was kinder on the score, but decided that 'it was difficult, under the depressing influence of the libretto and the lateness at which the performance concluded, to do justice to Signor Emilio Pizzi's music'.

PRO reference: COPY 1/123 folio 99
Artist: Arthur Benjamin Helsby
Printer: Weiner's Ltd
Registered: September 1895

Burlesque, Comic Opera and Musical Comedy

The Gay Parisienne

Northampton Opera House,
1 October 1894
Written by George Dance
Music by Ernest Vousden

Elephant and Castle Theatre,
23 March 1896
Written by George Dance
Music by Ivan Caryll

Duke of York's Theatre,
4 April 1896
Written by George Dance
Music by Ivan Caryll

The demurely veiled lady revealing a hint of lacy petticoat as she sits in her carriage is Mademoiselle Julie Bon-Bon, the 'Gay Parisienne' herself. This musical comedy was first produced in Northampton and toured in the provinces before coming to London with Ada Reeve in the title role. At last the newly-named Duke of York's Theatre experienced its first huge success as audiences enthusiastically encored *The Gay Parisienne*'s 'Cock-a-doodle-do' quartet and 'Tweedle-dee' duet.

The costumes, designed by Comelli, were the subject of an article in the ladies' page of *The Sketch*, where the writer thrilled in detail about the cut, colours, fabrics and flounces of Miss Reeves's two costumes, which she pronounced were 'equal to a dozen ordinary gowns'. The 'smart but practical attire' of the chorus of lady cyclists was also admired: dark-blue silk bloomers; white chiffon crevat blouses'; and straw hats 'jauntily trimmed' with Mercury wings. Cycling was a fashionable skill to acquire in the 1890s, and contemporary London theatre programmes carried advertisements for 'The Royal Cycle Schools' in the Euston Road, 'as patronised by Their Royal Highnesses the Princes of Siam'.

PRO reference: COPY 1/126
folio 372
Artist: Julius Mendes Price
Printer: Waterlow & Sons Ltd
Registered: April 1896

THE GEISHA
MR GEORGE EDWARDES' COMPANY

PLATE 10

The Geisha

Daly's Theatre, 25 April 1896

Book by Owen Hall
Music by Sidney Jones

The huge success of the comic opera *The Geisha* in London started a tremendous 'Geisha' craze, and before long manufacturers were producing all types of 'Geisha' products. At Daly's Theatre, Marie Tempest starred as the geisha girl O Mimosa San, while Letty Lind entranced audiences as the English girl who inadvertently became a geisha girl and was befriended by O Mimosa San. The impresario George Edwardes had known Letty Lind since her Gaiety Theatre days, when she had appeared in several productions including *Carmen Up To Data* [see plate 5]. Rutland Barrington – Pooh-Bah in the original production of *The Mikado* – was also in the cast.

Remembering the authentic detail of *The Mikado*'s sets and costumes, Edwardes employed the founder of the Japanese Society to oversee all details of the stage settings. He also commissioned one of the finest poster artists, Dudley Hardy, to design this poster, which reveals Hardy's delight in the colour, shape and decoration of the exotic kimono. This poster, and the excellent reputation of the London production, guaranteed crowded houses on the tour.

PRO reference: COPY 1/150 folio 100
Artist: Dudley Hardy
Printer: Waterlow & Sons Ltd
Registered: May 1899

PLATE 11

The Telephone Girl

Wolverhampton Grand, 25 May 1896
Metropole Theatre, Camberwell, 27 July 1896

Adapted from Desvallieres and Feydeau Libretto by Augustus Harris, F C Burnand and A Sturgess Music by Gaston Serpette and J M Glover

This had all the ingredients of a successful Gaiety piece – sparkling music and lyrics, contemporary settings, farcical situations, romantic comedy, and a 'girl' in the title.

The poster depicts Ada Blanche as Lottie Myrtle, the telephone operator, and also in her more risqué costume as 'Belle Bell, the Variety Sparkler'. Ada Blanche was best known as principal boy of Augustus Harris's spectacular pantomimes at Drury Lane [see *Cinderella*, plate 50].

Harris's name features prominently on this poster since his reputation for providing superb entertainment would have been an extra attraction.

PRO reference:
COPY 1/150 folio 89
Artist: Dudley Hardy
Printer: Waterlow & Sons Ltd
Registered: May 1899

Burlesque, Comic Opera and Musical Comedy

PLATE 12

Skipped by the Light of the Moon

*Reading County Theatre,
24 August 1896
Theatre Metropole,
5 April 1897*

*By George R Sims,
with lyrics by P Marshall
Music by Henry W May and
George Pack*

As this exuberant poster by
Dudley Hardy indicates, *Skipped
by the Light of the Moon* was
another generous helping of
attractively-dressed, frothy
musical entertainment. It was
written by George R Sims, the
author of *Faust Up To Date* and
Carmen Up To Data [see plates 3,
4 and 5]. Sims was a dramatist,
poet, author, social reformer and
journalist who also specialised in
melodrama, and it was perhaps
because his fame was greater than
that of the composers that their
names failed to feature on the
poster.

The plot of the piece concerns
two errant businessmen who
enjoy the delights of Brighton
while pretending to their wives
they are in the more genteel spot
of Shanklin. Act I is set in a
seaside hotel, and Act II in its
garden: the seaside theme gave
scope for a considerable number
of chorus members and dancers,
who appeared as waiters, golfers,
hotel visitors, seaside visitors,
minstrels and lady banjoists. The
cavorting chorus line shown here
are lady tennis players wielding
their racquets.

PRO reference: COPY 1/150
folio 106
Artist: Dudley Hardy
Printer: Waterlow & Sons Ltd
Registered: May 1899

PLATE 13

A Runaway Girl

Gaiety Theatre, 21 May 1898

Book by Seymour Hicks and
Harry Nicholls
Music by Ivan Caryll
and Lionel Monckton
Lyrics by Aubrey Hopwood
and Harry Greenbank

Most successful London productions could be seen on tour in the provinces in the 1890s, and this poster advertises a tour by George Edwardes' Company of yet another 'girl' production. It features the popular

high-kicking cancan dance seen against the picturesque Act II backdrop of Venice, where – as the chorus sang – 'the waterways sparkle at night / with lanterns and torches alike'. The style of William True's artwork as well as the dance has echoes of the posters of Toulouse-Lautrec, and from the poster hoardings it undoubtedly appealed to many a Victorian gentleman.

   The star of the piece in London was Ellaline Terriss, playing Winifred Grey, the 'runaway girl' who fled from a convent school in Corsica to join a troupe of

strolling musicians. Leading lady of the Gaiety's previous successes *My Girl* and *The Circus Girl*, Ellaline Terriss was the wife of one of the co-authors, Seymour Hicks. On tour at Plymouth in March 1899, her part was played by the Countess Russell – not the first time the aristocracy was associated with the Gaiety Theatre.

PRO reference: COPY 1/152
folio 126
Artist: Will. True
Printer: Waterlow & Sons Ltd
Registered: May 1899

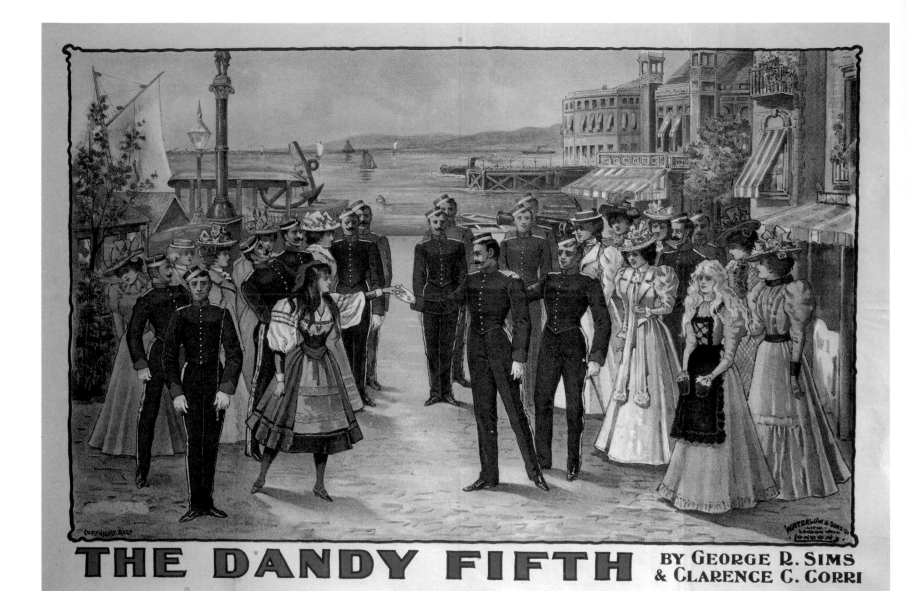

THE DANDY FIFTH BY GEORGE R. SIMS & CLARENCE C. CORRI

PLATE 14

The Dandy Fifth

Duke of York's Theatre, 16 August 1895
Prince of Wales's Theatre, Birmingham,
16 August 1898

By George R Sims
Music by Clarence C Corri

The stage set seen here may look like another view of the popular Venice, setting for *The Gondoliers* (1889), *The Bric-a-Brac Will* (1895), and *A Runaway Girl* (1898), but it was in fact 'Southsea Common, near the pier gates' – the location of Act I of *The Dandy Fifth*. This is where Kate Lorrimer, the General's daughter and well-bred heroine of this piece, encounters soldiers from the 5th Lancers (or 'The Dandy Fifth') when wearing Gypsy girl fancy dress costume. The gallant Dick Darville rescues her from their unwelcome attentions, and she is seen here stretching out her hand in gratitude. The course of their love does not run smoothly since she is also being courted by the Colonel, but two acts and many beautiful costumes later the united future of Kate and Dick is secure.

The libretto was by the prolific George R Sims, and despite praising it for a strong story-line, one critic was sardonic about its first-night reception in London: 'the applause was so indiscriminate as to provoke some reprisals on the part of the habitual playgoer, but beyond doubt many derived genuine amusement from the piece'.

PRO reference: COPY 1/150 folio 95
Artist: Sidney Ransom
Printer: Waterlow & Sons Ltd
Registered: May 1899

PLATE 15

Three Little Maids

*Apollo Theatre, 10 May 1902
Transferred to Prince of Wales's
Theatre, 8 September 1902*

*Written and composed by
Paul Rubens
Additional numbers by Howard
Talbot and Percy Greenbank*

Comic operas had successfully
visited exotic locations – Japan,
Venice, India, China, Spain – but
now George Edwardes and
Charles Frohman gave London a
very English comic opera, *Three
Little Maids*, starring Edna May,
Hilda Mooney and Madge
Crichton. They feature on the
poster in their roles as the
Reverend Branscombe's demure
daughters: Edna, Hilda and Ada.

Act I was set on the golf course
of the sleepy Surrey village of
Market Mallory; Act II in a smart
Bond Street tea shop, where the
girls become waitresses, and Act
III in Lady St Mallory's drawing
room, where the girls are invited
by their London beaux to a ball,
to be driven there in a motor car,
the very latest in fashionable
transport.

Reviewers praised its
refinement but regretted its
length and lack of vivacity:
'Restful this sort of piece may be
with its slight sentimental story,
its dainty love-songs, its few
graceful dances, but its duller
moments made the audience
yearn for the Gaiety's wilder fun,
more frolicking *pas-seuls* and
smarter ditties.'

PRO reference: COPY 1/98
folio 319
Artist: John Page
Printer: W T Haycock & Sons
Registered: December 1902

Burlesque, Comic Opera and Musical Comedy

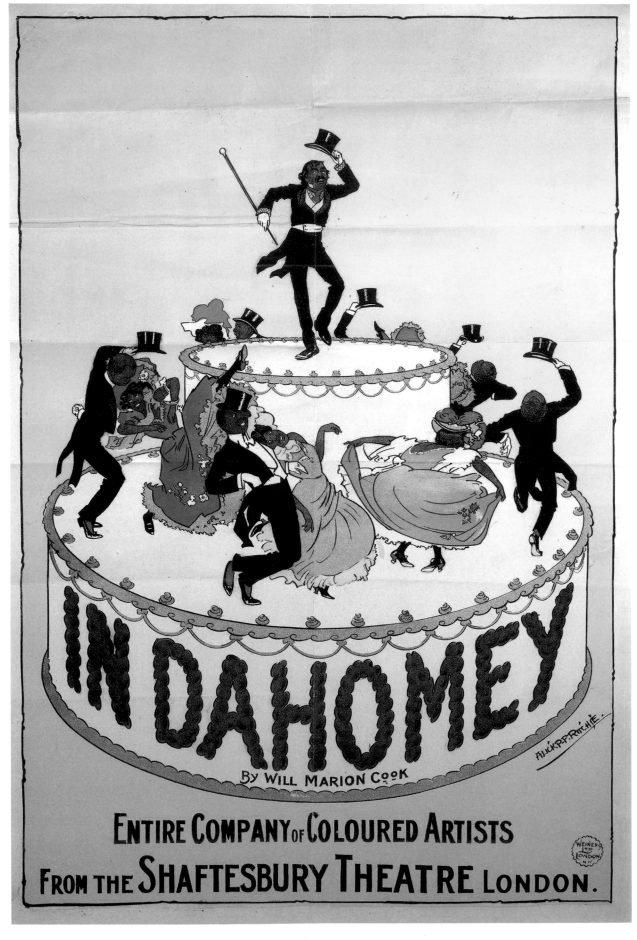

IN DAHOMEY

BY WILL MARION COOK

ENTIRE COMPANY OF COLOURED ARTISTS

FROM THE SHAFTESBURY THEATRE LONDON.

PLATE 16

In Dahomey

Shaftesbury Theatre,
16 May 1903

Written and staged by
Jesse A Shipp
Lyrics by Paul Lawrence Dunbar
and Alex Rogers
Composed by Will Marion Cook

This giant cake with its strutting dancers is inspired by the 'Cakewalk' number from *In Dahomey*, when characters at a Florida ball compete in a dancing competition for the prize of a cake. 'Sam Johnson's Cakewalk', originally performed by a troupe of black dancers in a musical in America in 1883, was already a popular dance on both sides of the Atlantic. In America, the Vanderbilts even had cakewalking lessons from George Walker, one of the stars of *In Dahomey*, while in London, cast members performed at Buckingham Palace and were in demand for cakewalking exhibitions at fashionable homes.

In Dahomey, an all-black musical comedy, was set in Boston, Florida and Dahomey, and concerned a syndicate in America promoting colonisation in the African kingdom of Dahomey. When they all decided to return to America, the cast sang the famous Victorian ballad, 'There's no place like home'. It was a refreshing novelty in London after years of minstrel shows, but it received more praise for its music and the energy and enthusiasm of its performers than for its lyrics and plot.

PRO reference: COPY 1/218 folio 273
Artist: Alick Penrose Ritchie
Printer: Weiner's Ltd
Registered: May 1904

PLATE 17

D'Oyly Carte Opera Company

No other company could produce better comic opera than the D'Oyly Carte Company, and perhaps no poster artist could produce better posters than John Hassall. The strongly delineated figure of the Mikado, from Gilbert and Sullivan's comic opera, grinning down from the poster hoardings, is an image that no passer-by could fail to notice.

The Mikado had been a huge success when first produced in London in 1885, and was constantly produced on tour by D'Oyly Carte's companies in the provinces and abroad. It was revived in London, at the Savoy Theatre, in 1896, and the character of the Mikado himself was readily associated by the public with the D'Oyly Carte Company.

When this poster was registered, in January 1905, the founder of the company, Richard D'Oyly Carte, was dead, but its management was ably continued by his wife, Helen. She commissioned this poster to advertise the company wherever they performed – as far afield as South Africa at the end of 1905. Helen D'Oyly Carte also showed sound business acumen by retaining the copyright of the poster.

PRO reference: COPY 1/226ii folio 191
Artist: John Hassall
Printer: Waterlow & Sons Ltd
Registered: January 1905

Burlesque, Comic Opera and Musical Comedy

PLATE 18

Amasis 'An Egyptian Princess'

New Theatre, 9 August 1906

Book by Frederick Fenn
Music by Philip Michael Faraday

Sebak, the keeper of the crocodiles (as played by Lauri de Frece), and Little Lilian, the crocodile, are wittily portrayed by John Hassall on this poster advertising the comic opera *Amasis*. Lilian wears a scarlet bow around her neck because of her status as a sacred animal.

The plot revolves around the love story of Princess Amasis, a daughter of the Pharaoh, and Prince Anhotep. The couple's plans to marry are thwarted by his inadvertently killing a cat, another sacred animal (like the crocodile and the ibis). Setting the opera in ancient Egypt meant that the designers could amaze audiences with the most marvellous sets and costumes, complete with pyramids, tombs and a chorus of 'Mummy Guards'.

Contemporary critics made flattering comparisons between this and the operas of Gilbert and Sullivan, and indeed, the part of the Pharaoh was played by the G&S star, Rutland Barrington. But unlike the works of Gilbert and Sullivan, *Amasis* is long forgotten, and the names of the author and the composer, Fenn and Faraday, have not achieved immortality.

PRO reference: COPY 1/274
folio 400
Artist: John Hassall
Printer: David Allen & Sons Ltd
Registered: October 1908

PLATE 19

The Private Secretary

Cambridge Theatre Royal,
14 November 1883
Prince's Theatre,
29 March 1884
Transferred to the Globe
Theatre, 19 May 1884

By C H Hawtrey, adapted from
Der Bibliothekar *by Von Moser*

The bumbling curate, the
Reverend Robert Spalding (seen
here laden down with luggage
and his beloved umbrella), was
the star of the farcical comedy
The Private Secretary. When first
produced in London at the
Prince's Theatre, Spalding was
played by Herbert Beerbohm
Tree, who later became one of the
most successful actor-managers of
his day and built Her Majesty's
Theatre in London's Haymarket.

The Private Secretary was
written by the actor-manager
Charles Hawtrey, who performed
in the Cambridge try-out but not
at the Prince's Theatre. After
critics gave it a lukewarm
reception, Hawtrey rejoined the
cast and transferred it to The
Globe, W S Penley replacing Tree.
Penley's rather doleful facial
expressions were perfect for the
part. The critic of *The Daily
Chronicle* wrote: 'As the timid
Robert Spalding, the curate who
is hustled about the stage almost
continuously, Mr Penley is as
funny as his predecessor, and he
has been endowed by nature with
certain attributes qualifying him
for the embodiment of such an
odd personage.'

The Private Secretary was a hit
at the Globe, where it ran until
1886, after which it toured and
was frequently revived, rivalling
even *Charley's Aunt* in popularity
[see plate 22].

PRO reference: COPY 1/71
folio 28
Artist: G H Knight
Printer: Clement-Smith & Co.
Registered: November 1885

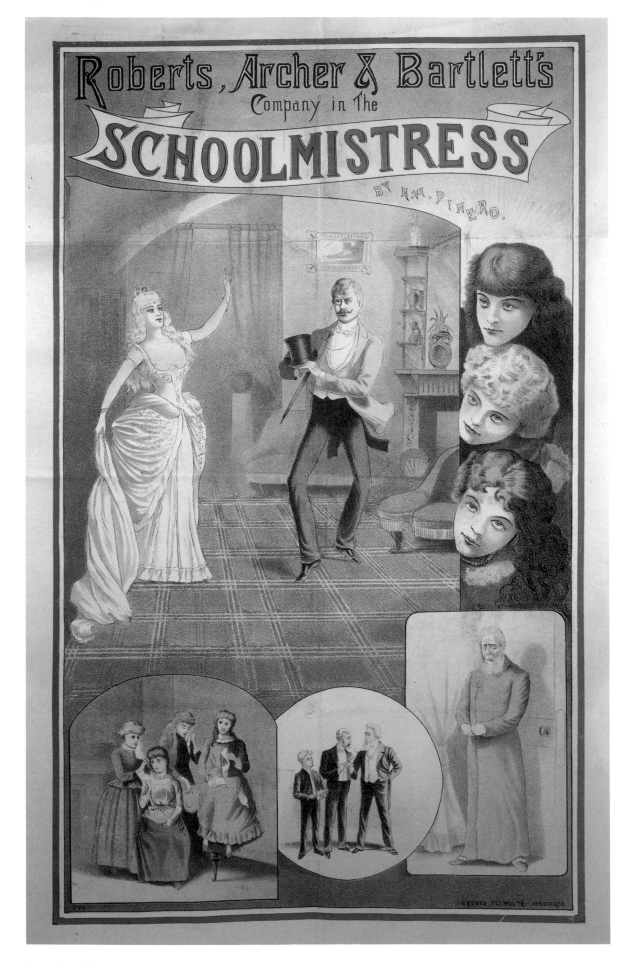

PLATE 20

The Schoolmistress

Court Theatre, 27 March 1886

By Arthur Wing Pinero

The style of this poster for the Roberts, Archer & Bartlett's Company tour of *The Schoolmistress* is not unusual, the artist depicting a selection of scenes and characters from the play.

However, the play – a 'farcical comedy' by Pinero – is one of the few productions featured in this book to have had a recent revival. Its plot was no less absurd than many contemporary farces, but its affectionate humour owed more to W S Gilbert than to the frantic French farces more usually adapted for the British stage in the 19th century.

Deception and confusion is its mainstay nevertheless: the story concerns three schoolgirls (one of them secretly married), and the principal of their boarding school, who also keeps her marriage a secret and whose clandestine occupation as a star of *opéra bouffe* has to be concealed from her husband. The girls are seen here peeping into the Act III moment when Miss Dycott defends her extra-mural activities to her husband: 'You *did* marry a lady! But scratch the lady and you find a hardworking comic actress!'

PRO reference: COPY 1/78
folio 249
Artist: Theophilus Creber
Printer: Theophilus Creber
Registered: May 1887

THE SOLICITOR

PLATE 21

The Solicitor

Liverpool Royal Court Theatre,
5 May 1890
Toole's Theatre, 3 July 1890

By J H Darnley

This moment of mayhem in a milliner's shop was the image chosen by the poster artist to attract audiences to the farce *The Solicitor* on tour. The incident is the climax of Act II: the respectable solicitor, Gilbert Brandon, emerges from concealment in a dress-stand; the Colonel's wife is embraced by the Captain; the Colonel is explaining himself to Mrs Brandon and Mrs Midhurst; the dressmaker has fainted in the arms of a young officer.

Even by contemporary standards of farce, the plot for *The Solicitor* was particularly ludicrous and complicated, including a stolen silver plate being driven to Shepherd's Bush by the solicitor, who has borrowed a hansom cab for a bet. Critics complained of 'a want of dramatic strength and sequence', but admitted that it had a lot of activity, with 'the opening and shutting of many doors, and the bustle of many people playing hide and seek'.

In London, the farce opened at Toole's Theatre in the Strand and was the first in a season of plays directed by Violet Melnotte, the manageress and theatre-owner who also staged *Erminie* [see plate 1].

PRO reference: COPY 1/111
folio 132
Artist: John Stewart Browne
Printed: David Allen & Sons Ltd
Registered: August 1890

PLATE 22

Charley's Aunt

*Bury St Edmund's Theatre,
29 February 1892
Royalty Theatre,
21 December 1892
Globe Theatre,
30 January 1893*

By Brandon Thomas

Charley's Aunt is depicted here as the Queen of Hearts, the globe as her sceptre. This symbolised her appearance at London's Globe Theatre, where the farce ran for four years, but also proved apt since *Charley's Aunt* became universally popular, was translated into many languages, and at one time was running simultaneously in forty-eight theatres throughout the world. Souvenirs of *Charley's Aunt* were legion, from dolls to paper knives, matchboxes to fans. No other play advertised by posters in this book became so popular or so lucrative.

Brandon Thomas wrote the play as a vehicle for W S Penley, the successful star of *The Private Secretary* [see plate 19]. Thomas was specific about the Aunt's costume, from 'the light brown wig parted in the centre and a bonnet of black silk with red roses' to 'the cameo brooch on a dress of stiff black satin worn over a black moiré silk petticoat'. Above all, he insisted that 'the Aunt must walk, talk and move like a man. There must be no vulgarity of scene or gesture.' Edward VII believed that the Aunt was a caricature of his mother, Queen Victoria, and refused to see the play.

PRO reference: COPY 1/124 folio 540
Artist: Chadwick Rymer
Printer: Weiner's Ltd
Registered: January 1896

PLATE 23

The Shadows on the Blind

Liverpool Prince of Wales Theatre, 27 September 1897
Terry's Theatre, 29 April 1898

By J H Darnley and H Bruce

The baby's milk is spilt, the baby's comforters are flying, and a man's silhouette is seen holding the baby ... This simple, four-colour image advertised *The Shadows on the Blind* at Terry's Theatre in the Strand, starring Edward Terry as the Professor of Chemistry, Adam Pemberton.

The effect of this poster is more menacing than that for *The Solicitor* [see plate 21], yet both were standard farces which would have come to nothing had the protagonists told the truth from the beginning. Poor Professor Pemberton finds himself like 'one man and a baby', spending an exhausting night trying to quieten an infant stranger, and the rest of the play managing its disappearance and concealing it from his wife and formidable mother-in-law.

British farces do not seem to have changed much in a hundred years. Even in 1898, one critic called it 'a very noisy, old-fashioned farce', adding cuttingly that it 'evoked a good deal of laughter, and may well amuse simple-minded playgoers'.

PRO reference: COPY 1/150
folio 86
Artist: Sidney Ransom
Printer: Waterlow & Sons Ltd
Registered: May 1899

TOMMY DODD

FROM THE

GLOBE THEATRE

WATERLOW & SONS Lᵗᵈ.
LITH.
LONDON WALL
LONDON

COPYRIGHT Rᵉᵍᵈ

Dudley Hardy

Comedy and Farce

PLATE 24

Tommy Dodd

*Cardiff Theatre Royal,
13 December 1897
Globe Theatre, 30 August 1898*

By Oscar Shillingford

There is a real sense of urgency and movement in this poster by Dudley Hardy, advertising the 1899 tour of *Tommy Dodd*. We only see the hindquarters of the galloping grey, his tail flying as his hooves and the coach wheels create a billowing swirl of dust. The comical coach driver looks bemused; the coach sways, and its occupant looks anxious as the furiously pedalling cyclist is gaining on them, complete with his unsuitably-dressed passenger. This was a poster promising an evening of excitement and action at the theatre!

Tommy Dodd was a farce named after the Honourable Thomas Dodd, a character who appears on stage very little, but with whom the heroine determines to elope when she discovers that her husband has married her under false pretences. The plot is tortuously complicated, with misunderstandings and disguises at every turn, but it was just what the public wanted. It was received enthusiastically at its first production in Cardiff in 1897, on its London transfer and subsequently on tour.

PRO reference: COPY 1/150 folio 108
Artist: Dudley Hardy
Printer: Waterlow & Sons Ltd
Registered: May 1899

PLATE 25

Beauty and the Barge

*New Theatre, 30 August 1904
Transferred to Haymarket
Theatre, 2 January 1905*

*By W W Jacobs and
Louis N Parker*

The cartoon-style graphics of the poster artist Tom Browne suit his subject perfectly. *Beauty and the Barge* was a farce based on the larger-than-life character Captain James Barley, who cannot tell a story without embellishing it. He comes to the rescue of Ethel Smedley, taking her to London on his barge since she is fleeing from the attentions of an unwelcome suitor. Ethel's other lover decides to go on the barge, too, disguised as the Mate, having persuaded the real one to feign illness. The rotund Mate's collapse is the incident shown here.

This production was a success in London, with Cyril Maude as the Captain, Lennox Pawle as the Mate and Mary Brough as Ethel. Maude's Company began touring the farce in 1905, when this poster was registered. Browne designed several posters for this tour and retained the copyright of their designs.

Nautical stories were stock-in-trade for the co-author of the play, W W Jacobs, the son of a Wapping wharf manager whose first volume of sea stories, *Many Cargoes*, had been published in 1896. He was better known, later, for his horror stories, including *The Monkey's Paw. Beauty and the Barge* was his first play, written in collaboration with the experienced playwright, Louis Parker.

PRO reference: COPY 1/225
folio 547
Artist: Tom Browne
Printer: not noted
Registered: December 1905

PLATE 26

Never Despair

Gaiety Theatre, Halifax, 5 May 1887
Sadler's Wells Theatre, 9 March 1889

By George Comer

A full moon above St Paul's Cathedral gleams on the Thames, but in contrast to this tranquillity, gunshots are fired. Spriggins and Ben Brierly have come by boat to rescue Kate and Harry, the lovers imprisoned in a house in old Southwark. Realistic representation of this scene on stage would have been difficult, but on

Thomas Phillips's poster it looked sensational.

This melodrama was originally presented by Reginald Patterson's touring company, with Albert Patterson in the cast, and thus their names feature here rather than that of the author, George Comer. Comer specialised in sensational melodrama: two days after this began, another of his intricately plotted works opened at London's Sanger's Theatre.

With one murder, two attempted murders, three incidents of drugging, plus schemes to deport Harry and to drive him

insane, one critic described *Never Despair* as 'that sort of piece in which the hurried action and stirring incident leave the spectator no time for reflection'. Its success on tour was followed two years later by a London production at Sadler's Wells Theatre.

PRO reference: COPY 1/79
folio 72
Artist: Thomas Phillips
Printer: Stafford & Co.
Registered: July 1887

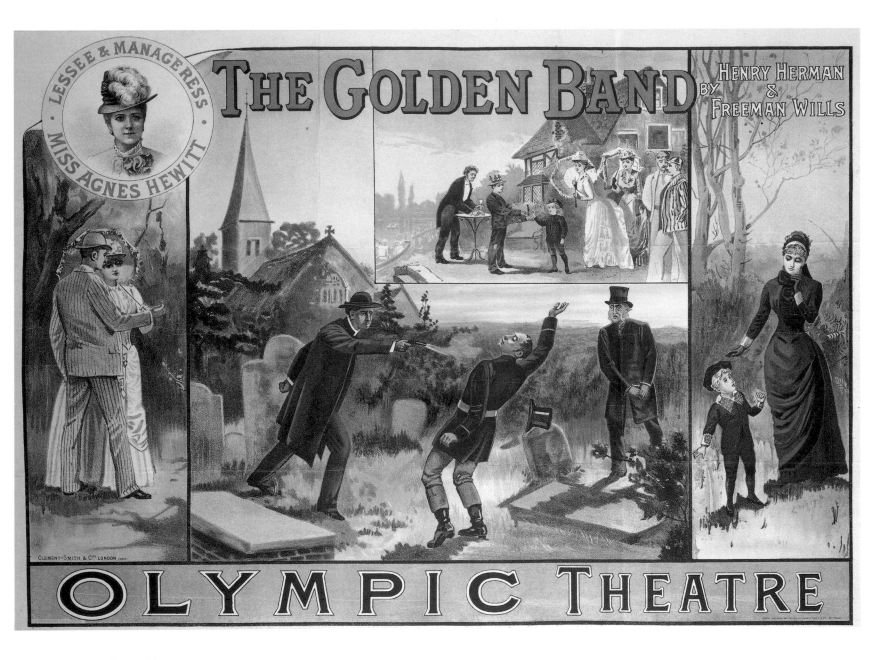

PLATE 27

The Golden Band

Olympic Theatre, 14 June 1887

By Henry Herman and Freeman Wills

London's Olympic Theatre suffered from a run of unsuccessful productions in the 1880s, and was dubbed by one critic the 'unlucky Olympic'. *The Golden Band* did little to restore its fortunes. It was brimming with intrigue and incident, but its desperately complicated plot left the audience more confused than amused.

Spoilt for choice, the artist included several scenes from the melodrama here, adding a portrait of the theatre's lessee for good measure. The main image shows the murder of Detective Grainger in the churchyard by the villainous counterfeit clergyman William Orchardy, while Orchardy's equally reprehensible uncle stands by, handcuffed by Grainger. Above, we see the Thames-side inn scene, while on the right, the dispossessed heroine, Ellen, walks with her son.

The play ended happily, unlike Agnes Hewitt's career as a theatrical entrepreneur.

Running a theatre was an expensive luxury, and by March 1889 she was declared bankrupt, unable to pay the Olympic's rent of £60 a week and £1,400 in arrears. By December 1889, she had reverted to acting in other people's productions [see plate 52, *Jack and the Beanstalk*].

PRO reference: COPY 1/79
folio 142
Artist: Harry Tuck
Printer: Clement-Smith & Co.
Registered: July 1887

PLATE 28

Shadows of a Great City

*First produced in America
Glasgow Princess's Theatre,
28 February 1887
Princess's Theatre,
14 July 1887*

*By Joseph Jefferson
and L R Sherwell*

Dastardly doings are afoot. Two escaped convicts in striped prison uniforms are abducting an infant heiress whom one of them plans to kill. Luckily, the other convict is really a gallant British sailor who rescues her and, fifteen years later, falls in love with her and marries her, once she is released from incarceration in a safe!

Such was the improbable plot of this American melodrama first performed at the Princess's Theatre by British actors who failed dismally at producing convincing American accents.

Reviews could hardly have been worse, yet the public loved it. One critic said it was 'calculated to shatter the lingering relics in the belief in drama as a form of entertainment', while another called it 'a flashy mixture of things new and old, extravagant and improbable' and said scathingly that it was 'accepted as both strange and wonderful by the gaping, wide-mouthed cousins and honest yokels who crowd to London during the excursion-train season'.

PRO reference: COPY 1/79
folio 73
Artist: Thomas Phillips
Printer: Stafford & Co.
Registered: July 1887

The Slave Girl

Avenue Theatre,
22 February 1892
(as Deborah*)*
Bristol Princess's
Theatre,
26 September 1893

By Langdon Elwyn
Mitchell

Deborah the slave heroine is helpless, bound by both wrists to a tree by the wicked overseer, Crawford. 'She is a woman!' 'She is a slave!' She is also about to be rescued by Bastien St Michael, the son of the owner of the American plantation where Deborah has been forced to work. Bastien, however, proves to be a coward and a cad: when his father mortally wounds Deborah, father and son leave the scene. Deborah dies alone as the curtain falls.

After its first production in London, *Deborah* became *The Slave Girl*, perhaps to disassociate itself from some dreadful first-night reviews. Isabel Bateman was the youngest daughter of a well-known theatrical family. She formed her own touring company, and saw potential for her talents in the character of this heroine.

PRO reference:
COPY 1/112
folio 81
Artist: Albert Morrow
Printer: David Allen &
Sons Ltd
Registered: March 1894

THE **MARINERS** OF **ENGLAND**

or the DAYS OF NELSON.

"*Your Sword, Sir!*"

THE *GREAT NAVAL HISTORICAL DRAMA* FROM THE **OLYMPIC THEATRE, LONDON.**

PLATE 30

The Mariners of England

*Nottingham Grand Theatre,
1 March 1897
Olympic Theatre,
9 March 1897*

*By Robert Buchan and
Charles Marlowe
(pseudonym of Harriet Jay)*

This was stirring stuff indeed – a 'romantic drama in four acts and two tableaux' guaranteed to bring a patriotic tear to the eye of all true Englishmen in the audience. For its plot, the authors looked back to 1805, the year of the Battle of Trafalgar. In Act I, on the cliffs at Dover, they introduce the heroic young British sailor, Harry Dell. Around him, his sweet foster-sister, Mabel, and the brave Lord Nelson, they tell a tale of villainy and duplicity involving the attempted assassination of Nelson by the aristocratic Captain Lebaudy and John Marston, a spy in the pay of France.

The scene shown here takes place in Lord Nelson's state cabin on HMS *Victory*, the setting for Act III. With Captain Hardy looking on, Nelson charges the cowardly Lebaudy with his crimes, demanding the surrender of his sword. There is just a suggestion of the Union Jack in the foreground.

The 'tableaux' of the play were recreations of the Battle of Trafalgar and the Death of Lord Nelson, great set-pieces in every sense, which drew enthusiastic applause.

PRO reference: COPY 1/239
folio 105
Artist: Will. True
Printer: David Allen & Sons Ltd
Registered: January 1906

Woman and Wine

Pavilion Theatre,
11 October 1897
Princess's Theatre, 8 March 1899

By Ben Landeck and
Arthur Shirley

This wonderfully effervescent poster advertised the tour of the 'romantic and spectacular drama' *Woman and Wine*, originally produced in London at the Whitechapel Pavilion Theatre, 11 October 1897, and revived at the Princess's Theatre in March, 1899. Dudley Hardy's design depicts a woman as a peacock, her patterned dress billowing like its iridescent tail. But she is obviously 'a bad lot' – she smokes and is dominated by the champagne which pours from her glass. She is the play's unscrupulous French character, Marcelle Rigadout – 'the woman who didn't care' – who tricks the wholesome hero, Dick Seymour, into deserting his sweetheart to live with her in Paris as her lover.

The play features a knife battle to the death between Marcelle and another female character from the underworld, both stripped to their bodices and petticoats. It shocked the reviewer of the original production, who nevertheless conceded that its 'Zola-like realism will win it much favour' and that it 'appeals effectively to the East-ender'.

PRO reference: COPY 1/150
folio 85
Artist: Dudley Hardy
Printer: Waterlow & Sons Ltd
Registered: May 1899

Drama and Melodrama

DAVID ALLEN & SONS LTD
17 LEICESTER ST
LONDON W
HARROW · BELFAST · MANCHESTER ·
GLASGOW & DUBLIN
(Copyright 1906)

PLATE 32

The French Spy

Morton's Theatre, Greenwich,
5 March 1900

By E Hill-Mitchelson

This was a story of espionage, murder and treachery from the playwright of *Rogues and Vagabonds*, *The Terror of Paris* and *Death or Glory Boys*. The titles speak for themselves, and the public loved them.

The French spy of this play is Countess André, in St Petersburg to steal the draft of an important treaty from the British Embassy. She is assisted by the unprincipled nobleman Count Romanoff, who means to leave his wife, Olga, to marry the Countess.

The most picturesque of the five acts was that set in a variety theatre in the Tivoli Gardens, when the strong man, Fritz, helps the unfortunate Olga to escape to Germany. Vignettes from this act are shown on the poster, giving the artist an opportunity to show the charms of the variety artiste as well as the might of Fritz. Fritz was played by Fred Benton, whose company performed the play at Greenwich, and later on tour.

PRO reference: COPY 1/240
folio 297
Artist: Arthur Brooke White
Printer: David Allen & Sons Ltd
Registered: January 1906

Sherlock Holmes

Based on A Conan Doyle's novel The Strange Case of Miss Faulkner

First produced in America Liverpool Shakespeare Theatre, 2 September 1901 Lyceum Theatre, 9 September 1901

By A Conan Doyle and William Gillette

The artist of this poster also designed the posters advertising *Erminie* [plate 1] and *The Solicitor* [plate 21]. For this design, registered during the tour, Browne restricted his palette to red and black, with striking results. Holmes has a rather pained expression but is probably contemplating his struggle to outwit Professor Moriarty and recover the Count's love letters written to Miss Faulkner.

Despite the more contemporary style of the poster, the production was a melodrama, but written with more real suspense and subtlety than was usual. When first seen at the Lyceum Theatre, the public were dismayed by the novelty of dimming the auditorium lights when the lamp on stage was smashed, and playing some of the escape scene in almost total darkness.

The American actor William Gillette originally brought this to England in 1901, and in 1905 the American impresario Charles Frohman organised its tour.

PRO reference: COPY 1/232 folio 424
Artist: John Stewart Browne
Printer: David Allen & Sons Ltd
Registered: August 1905

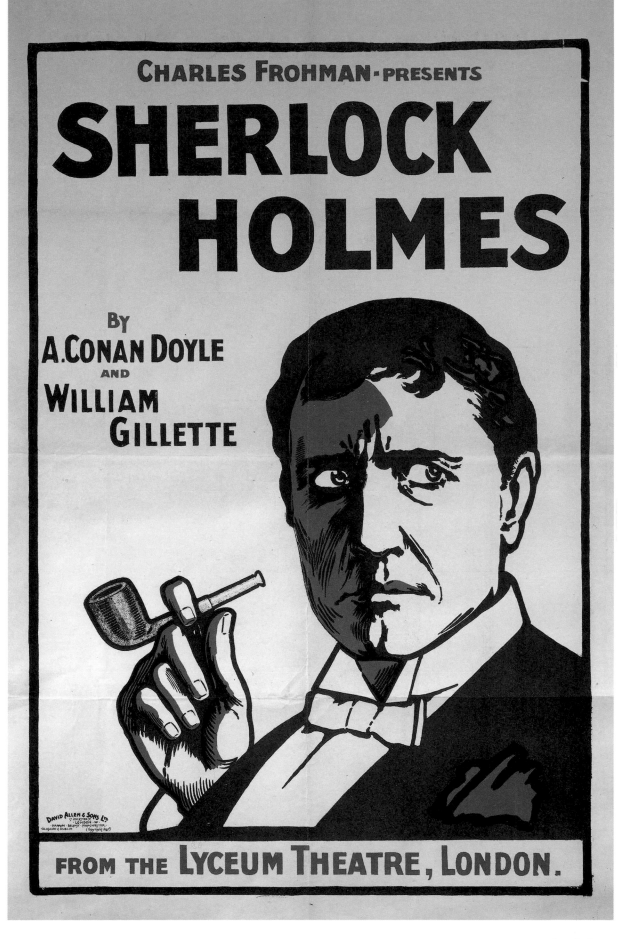

PLATE 34

On the Rocks

By Cayley Calvert

Authors of melodramas vied with each other to find the most dramatic and picturesque settings. Locating his 'romantic and dramatic sketch' in a lighthouse on a remote island meant that Cayley Calvert could show his characters in isolation, struggling for their lives against the villain of the piece. Brave Jack proved more than a match for *him*, however, and despite the struggle in the lighthouse shown on the poster, it all ended happily. Audiences loved the action and the excitement, even with lines like: 'There stands the man who pushed him over!'

This was not a full-length melodrama, but instead, a piece which may have lasted about forty minutes. Charles Jackson's Company would have toured with it round the country, presenting it as one item during a long evening's entertainment at variety theatres, travelling with their backcloth, properties and band parts for the resident orchestra. Charles Jackson would have purchased the rights to present it from the author, and it was he who commissioned the poster artist, registered the poster and retained its copyright.

PRO reference: COPY 1/178 folio 2
Artist: Emil Paul Fischer
Printer: not noted
Registered: May 1901

Drama and Melodrama

PLATE 35

The Great Millionaire

Theatre Royal, Drury Lane,
19 September 1901

By Cecil Raleigh
Incidental music by J M Glover

By the turn of the century, the Theatre Royal at Drury Lane was famous for its spectacular 'autumn dramas', featuring crowds of performers, realistic sets, thrilling plots and music and at least one big 'sensation'. On this tour poster the 'sensation' of *The Great Millionaire* is shown – the moment when the Gypsy, Isaac Grant, tries to throttle Digby Grant at the wheel, thus diverting him from his intended route to Plymouth.

This melodrama, originally produced at Drury Lane on 19 September 1901, boasted ninety-one performers and cost over £10,000 to mount. A real £700 motor car was used on stage, but its fatal descent was simulated by cinematic means 'by the British Muroscope and Biograph Company'.

The Theatre Royal had undergone extensive renovations immediately before *The Great Millionaire* opened, and its hydraulically operated bridges could raise and lower parts of the stage to enhance effects. On tour, effects were scaled down to suit the less technically advanced theatres where it appeared.

PRO reference: COPY 1/220ii
folio 6
Artist: Edward Patrick Kinsella
Printer: David Allen & Sons Ltd
Registered: September 1904

PLATE 36

If I Were King

St James's Theatre,
30 August 1902

By Justin Huntley McCarthy

This poster features the slim figure of the actor-manager George Alexander in his Act I costume as François Villon, the 15th-century French poet on whom this play was based. The lamp-lit face and dark shadow convey a sense of mystery but give no hint of the huge scale of the production.

No money was spared on this four-act 'romantic play', complete with overture, incidental music, a Gypsy ballet, thirty speaking parts and at least as many extras playing ladies, courtiers, knights, monks, archers, soldiers, citizens, peasants, torchbearers and attendants. The many sets and costumes were by well-known artists, and when Villon proved his worth as substitute king in battle with the Duke of Burgundy, he was accompanied on stage by a large grey horse. As the commentator of the magazine *The Playgoer* noted, 'everything is done on the cost-it-what-it-may principle, to which playgoers of late have become accustomed'.

The play was a success, as was George Alexander's tenure of the St James's Theatre. The play celebrated its 200th performance on 26 February 1903, and in 1911 George Alexander was honoured with a knighthood.

PRO reference: COPY 1/198
folio 64
Artist: Charles ('Chas') Buchel
Printer: Waterlow & Sons Ltd
Registered: December 1902

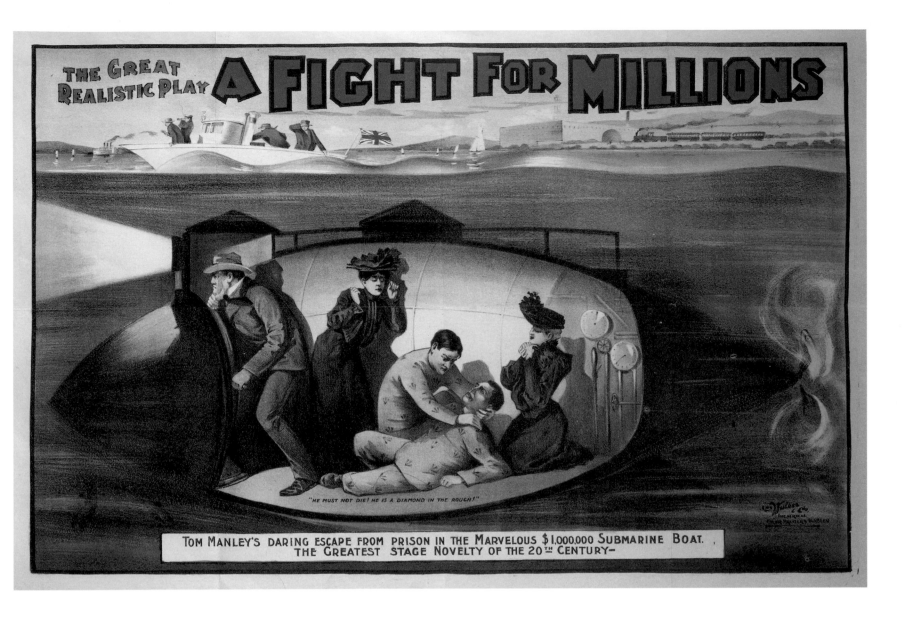

THE GREAT REALISTIC PLAY **A FIGHT FOR MILLIONS**

"HE MUST NOT DIE! HE IS A DIAMOND IN THE ROUGH!"

TOM MANLEY'S DARING ESCAPE FROM PRISON IN THE MARVELOUS $1,000,000 SUBMARINE BOAT.
THE GREATEST STAGE NOVELTY OF THE 20TH CENTURY—

PLATE 37

A Fight for Millions

Coliseum, Oldham, 11 January 1904
Greenwich, Carlton, 15 February 1904

By Malcolm Douglas

Plots hardly came more complicated and fantastic than this. The villain of this American melodrama, Richard Dudley, ingratiates himself with his employer, Hudson Rivers, so that Rivers makes a will leaving Dudley $5 million and his daughter in marriage. Pearl, the daughter in question, objects to the arrangement,

not least because of her love for Tom Manley, the inventor of a 'wireless ocean telephone'. Dudley's deserted wife and child also prove problematic and thwart his attempt to blow up a train on which Rivers is travelling. Eventually, Dudley shoots Rivers and implicates Manley, who is imprisoned and sentenced to death. This scene takes place after Manley has escaped from prison by chloroforming the warders and scaling the walls. Luckily, Mrs Rivers has a submarine constructed for his escape, and it is in this that Manley's

wireless ocean telephone comes into its own.

Each new, thrilling twist of plot was received vociferously by audience members, and at Greenwich they longed to get at the evil Dudley, 'but fortunately the footlights intervened'!

PRO reference: COPY 1/211
folio 98
Artist: Robert Ferris
Printer: James Walker & Co.
Registered: January 1904

PLATE 38

Her Forbidden Marriage

Terriss Theatre, Rotherhithe, 4 April 1904

By Frederick Melville

Devereux bursts into the church where Lucy and Maddison stand at the altar, defying the dictates of her guardian. As Lucy cries 'send him away', her hated erstwhile suitor, Devereux, declaims: 'Lucy is not your wife yet, and never shall be; I forbid you to continue this service, you shall never marry.' The Minister replies: 'too late, they are already man and wife!' Church bells start to ring, and the curtain falls on Act II.

Lucy is in a convent when Act III opens, already having borne a child by Maddison, from whom she is now cruelly separated by his false imprisonment. Action moved fast in melodrama by the Melvilles, and created stage pictures that were a gift for the poster artist, even if William Morgan's skills as a poster artist did not make the most of them. Since this poster was used for the tour, William Morgan would probably have seen the production when it was originally presented at the Terriss Theatre, Rotherhithe, one of the theatres where Walter and Frederick Melville were based.

PRO reference: COPY 1/242i folio 179
Artist: William Edward Morgan
Printer: David Allen & Sons
Registered: March 1906

Drama and Melodrama

PLATE 39

A Disgrace to Her Sex

*Terriss Theatre, Rotherhithe,
23 May 1904*

By Walter Melville

Blackmail, assumed identity, theft,
drunkenness, an illegitimate child,
thwarted love – all the necessary
ingredients of a Melville melodrama
which delighted audiences of
A Disgrace to Her Sex.

The tour poster shows
highlights of the action. Beneath
the title, the shameful woman,
Hilda Valley, casts her eyes to the
floor in contrition while the two
men she has deceived gaze at her
with concern. In the central
image, she begs Carrington's
forgiveness, while on either side
we see Carrington's two daughters
– 'one born in wedlock, the other
born in shame' – being kissed.
Then there is David Carrington's
birthmark, which establishes his
true identity, and the fight in the
courtyard of the Royal Court Inn.
All this went down well with
audiences when the play was
originally presented at the
Terriss Theatre, Rotherhithe, on
30 March 1904, and when it was
taken on tour.

PRO reference: COPY 1/242i
folio 173
Artist: William Edward Morgan
Printer: David Allen & Sons Ltd
Registered: March 1906

PLATE 40

The Ugliest Woman on Earth

Terriss Theatre, Rotherhithe, 14 November 1904

By Frederick Melville

Posters for melodramas by the Melville brothers were not remarkable for artistic excellence, but they were graphic, often huge, and always featured the plays' sensational titles in large lettering, as on this tour poster for *The Ugliest Woman on Earth*. Posters like this attracted full houses in London and in the provinces, where the Melvilles sent as many as twenty-five touring companies at once to present their plays. Despite claims from many critics that melodrama had had its day by 1904, there were still thousands of people who wanted to come to a Melville melodrama to cheer the heroine and hiss the villain.

This play opened at the Terriss Theatre in Rotherhithe in November 1904 and features a doctor and his assistant, a mysteriously veiled woman who is travelling in Italy with him. An illness has disfigured her face so much that she hides it. When the hero, Jack Merriman, is blinded by villains, she confesses her love for him and they marry, their love restoring both his sight and her beauty.

PRO reference: COPY 1/242i
folio 183
Artist: William Edward Morgan
Printer: David Allen & Sons Ltd
Registered: March 1906

Drama and Melodrama

The Whip

Theatre Royal, Drury Lane,
9 September 1909

By Cecil Raleigh and
Henry Hamilton

Drury Lane cornered the market in sensational melodrama – the bigger the better. The 'sporting drama', *The Whip*, was its most ambitious to date, a huge success which ran for 388 performances. On stage, the racehorse – 'The Whip' – is rescued in the nick of time from a horsebox uncoupled from a train by villains. The following train rushes from a tunnel to crash into the horsebox, smashing it to smithereens before turning on its side, belching steam. The finale is the Two Thousand Guineas race at Newmarket, with horses galloping on stage using the 'reverse escalator' system.

The huge stage of Drury Lane was equipped with hydraulic lifts which made the complex scenic engineering possible. The original Drury Lane Company took the production to America, while George Dance toured it in Britain, scaled-down for less scenically-advanced stages. This poster was used on tour.

In 1917 the melodrama inspired the full-length silent film *The Whip*, produced in America by Paragon Films, directed by Maurice Tourneur.

PRO reference: COPY 1/317
folio 295
Artist: Albert Morrow
Printer: David Allen & Sons Ltd
Registered: January 1912

ALDWYCH THEATRE
STRAND, W. C.

GENERAL MANAGER   Mr ALBERT ARCHDEACON.

MISS ALEXANDRA CARLISLE
as
PROUD MAISIE

PLATE 42

Proud Maisie

*Aldwych Theatre,
12 March 1912*

By Edward G Hemmerde

Inspired by Scottish ancestral portraits painted in bosky lochside settings, this poster depicts Alexandra Carlisle as Lady Maisie Monteith, the romantic heroine of *Proud Maisie.* The play is set in Pitcour Castle in 1745, and was inspired by the poem 'Proud Maisie' by Sir Walter Scott. Despite its atmospheric sets, picturesque costumes and authentic music, the play was not a palpable hit.

The cast featured some well-known actors, notably Leon Quartermaine as Maisie's brother, Guy Monteith, and Henry Ainley as her lover, Neil MacAlpine, but audiences did not respond to its heroic blank verse or its tragic plot, 'full of the spirit of valour, love, nobility and self-sacrifice'. This was *Romeo and Juliet* in kilts: after Proud Maisie takes the place of her twin brother in a sword-fight and is killed by her lover, he immediately stabs himself in remorse over her dead body. The hapless lovers are carried off, wrapped in plaid, to the mournful music of the pipes.

PRO reference: COPY 1/319 folio 37
Artist: Sidney Freshfield
Printer: Haycock-Cadle Co.
Registered: March 1912

PLATE 43

**The Golden Land
of Fairy Tales**

*Aldwych Theatre,
14 December 1911*

*Translated and adapted by
A H Quaritch and Maurice Raye
Music by Heinrich Berte*

Good, wholesome family
entertainment was on offer at the
Aldwych Theatre for Christmas
1911 – 'a feast for little ones
and their elders!' As this poster
indicated, there was no danger
here of any unsuitable references
in this seasonal entertainment.

This poster design is more
like a book illustration with its
dancing fairy tale characters and
enraptured youngsters listening
to their storytelling granny.
Indeed, it echoes the frontispiece
illustration to Charles Perrault's
Contes de ma Mère l'Oye in
which the 17th-century Frenchman
collected and published (for the
first time) eight traditional French
fairy tales. But the poster would
also have appealed to children in
1911, for whom the production
was intended as a Christmas
treat. The performance began
with a prologue by the narrator,
Granny, followed by six fairy
tale 'tableaux', with music and
dancing, much of which was
done by children.

Picture books came to life
in this production which even
included a tableau recreating
a Burne-Jones painting in
'The Sleeping Beauty' scene.
'The 'Grand Finale' was described
as 'a Vision of the Golden Land,
with the Queen Fairy, the Fairy
Ballet and the Children who have
been made happy by fairy tales'.
One reviewer noted sardonically:
'*The Golden Land of Fairy Tales*
made me feel frightfully old!'

PRO reference: COPY 1/319
folio 38
Artist: Val Prince
Printer: Haycock-Cadle Co.
Registered: March 1912

Children's Plays and Pantomime

CREBER, PLYMOUTH.

PLATE 44

Aladdin

Stock poster issued by Creber c.1886

The design and the figure drawing on this poster leave much to be desired, but as a stock poster promising curtailed costumes and scenic splendour, it probably served its purpose. We see menacing faces in the rock, a dragon-shaped lamp fizzing promisingly, and an Aladdin whose pose reveals amazement at the tidings of an obviously good fairy.

Aladdin first trod the pantomime boards at the Theatre Royal, Covent Garden, on Boxing Day 1788. The story was taken from the *Arabian Nights* and featured an African magician who was christened Abanazer in a non-pantomimic version at the Theatre Royal, Covent Garden, in 1813. By the 1880s, when this poster was produced, *Aladdin* was already one of the most popular pantomimes, complete with Widow Twankay, who entered the scene in 1861, named after Twankay tea imported to Britain from China.

PRO reference: COPY 1/76 folio 422
Artist: Theophilus Creber
Printer: Creber & Co.
Registered: December 1886

PLATE 45

Babes in the Wood

Stock poster issued by
Stafford & Co. c.1886

The Babes lie on the ground
while the wood is filled with
robins bringing leaves to
cover them. The robins are
probably shown here
protecting the sleeping babes,
but in harsher versions of
the pantomime, staged in
London in 1827 and in 1856,
the babes perished and the
robins covered their dead
bodies.

This supposedly true
story was first dramatised
in the 18th century, taken
from the ballad *The Children
in the Wood*, or, *The Norfolk
Gentleman's Last Will and
Testament*, registered in
Stationers' Hall in 1595.
It concerns a widower from
Watton in Norfolk, who on
his deathbed gives his
brother charge of his two
infant children and all his
money. To secure the fortune
for himself the uncle leaves
them to die in Wayland Wood,
but the children survive and
it is the uncle who perishes,
in prison. By 1867, the tale
of the babes was embellished
by the characters from the
Robin Hood story that we
commonly find in the
pantomime today.

PRO reference: COPY 1/76
folio 421
Artist: Thomas Phillips
Printer: Stafford & Co.
Registered: December 1886

Children's Plays and Pantomime

PLATE 46

Dick Whittington

Stock poster issued by Creber c.1889

Like the poster for *Babes in the Wood* [plate 45], this was a stock poster which could be purchased by any management staging the pantomime. The artist doubtless emphasised the curvaceous qualities of the principal boy, but the costumes and corsets worn by the ladies who played these roles did much to create a similar effect on stage.

Samuel Pepys recorded seeing a puppet play based on Whittington in 1668, but it was first staged as a pantomime in 1814 at the Theatre Royal, Covent Garden, as *Harlequin Whittington, or, the Lord Mayor of London*. Since then, Dick and his cat have perennially sought fame and fortune on the pantomime stage.

PRO reference: COPY 1/88
folio 506
Artist: Theophilus Creber
Printer: Creber
Registered: December 1889

PLATE 47

Robinson Crusoe

Stock poster

Daniel Defoe's novel, *Robinson Crusoe*, was first staged as a pantomime at the Theatre Royal, Drury Lane, in January 1781. Called *Robinson Crusoe*, or, *Harlequin Friday*, it was written by Richard Brinsley Sheridan, author of *The Rivals* and *The Critic*. Sheridan was lampooned for sinking to such a low form of entertainment, but it was a great success.

By the 1880s, *Robinson Crusoe* was a favourite pantomime, regularly performed all over the country each Christmas, and printers found it worthwhile to produce the title as a stock poster. Managements who could not go to the expense of commissioning posters found it useful to be able to buy stock posters, overprinting details of their production on the yellow strip at the top. Since all pantomimes aspired to being 'gorgeous', the printers could safely issue the posters with that adjective in place.

PRO reference: COPY 1/76 folio 133
Artist: Thomas Phillips
Printer: Stafford & Co.
Registered: December 1886

PLATE 48

The Babes in the Wood

*Manchester Theatre Royal,
20 December 1883*

*By Mr E Edmonds
Music arranged by John Crook*

As indicated by its full title, *Harlequin Happy-Go-Lucky and the Babes in the Wood* featured a final harlequinade with Clown, Columbine, Harlequin, Policeman and Pantaloon involved in a farcical chase. The story was based on the traditional English tale of babes left in a wood to die by their uncle, but the narrative was of marginal importance amidst a feast of changing scenes. These ranged from the Animated Nursery and Haunted Bedchamber to a Balloon Ascent into Cloudland (featuring panoramic views of Manchester), and a Grand Transformation scene of 'The Robins' Christmas Time' lit by a burst of electric lighting provided by the Edison Electric Light Company. Since this illumination was such a novelty, Electra was one of the fairy characters, punningly described in the programme as 'rather light-headed, although his Edison the right way'. Drury Lane's *Cinderella* similarly featured a fairy Electra in their 1883 pantomime.

The Babes were played by the children Katie and Mabel Grattan; there was a wicked Demon, and a comic Baroness played by Mr W F Hawtrey. The 'dashing youth', Happy-Go-Lucky, who follows the Babes through their adventures was played by Miss Jenny Hill, a popular music hall star whose presence attracted audiences much as a sport or television personality does in pantomime today.

PRO reference: COPY 1/110i
folio 566
Artist: Charles Norris Cooper
Printer: C A Corner
Registered: November 1893

Children's Plays and Pantomime

PLATE 49

Cinderella

*Theatre Royal, Drury Lane,
26 December 1895*

*By Sir Augustus Harris,
Cecil Raleigh and
Arthur Sturgess
Music by J M Glover*

Cinderella, as played by
Isa Bowman, looks demurely
over her shoulder and lifts her
gown to reveal a dainty ankle
and the fabled glass slipper.
With her ostrich feather fan
and plumes in her hair, the
artist depicts her in the costume
designed by the prolific Victorian
designer, Comelli.

By 1895, Drury Lane Theatre
was known as the home of
glamorous pantomime,
sumptuously mounted by
Sir Augustus Harris. He had
been manager of the theatre
since 1879, and for this
Cinderella, returned to the
earlier fairy tale extravaganza
style, aiming to diminish the
increasingly intrusive 'variety
element'.

Harris spared no expense on
publicity, and for this production
also commissioned a huge poster
by the Beggarstaff Brothers, and
another by Dudley Hardy [see
plate 50]. This was to be Harris's
last pantomime at Drury Lane,
since he died in June 1896, aged
forty-four.

PRO reference: COPY 1/123
folio 201
Artist: Arthur Benjamin Helsby
Printer: Weiners Ltd
Registered: December 1895

PLATE 50

Cinderella

*Theatre Royal,
Drury Lane,
26 December 1895*

*By Sir Augustus
Harris, Cecil Raleigh
and Arthur Sturgess
Music by J M Glover*

The flunkeys bow their heads obsequiously as Cinderella, the 'grande dame', sweeps up the red-carpeted staircase. The success of Hardy's 1893 poster for *A Gaiety Girl* at London's Prince of Wales's Theatre had established his reputation and his services were much in demand.

His first poster had been commissioned by Augustus Harris, and it was Harris who asked him to design a poster for this spectacular version of *Cinderella*, in which Cinderella goes to the ball in a jewelled motor carriage with a large wheel blazing with electric light in the background. Dan Leno played the Baroness to Herbert Campbell's Baron with Isa Bowman as Cinderella and Ada Blanche and Alexandra Dagmar in the 'tights' roles of the Prince and Dandini.

PRO reference:
COPY 1/150 folio 88
Artist: Dudley Hardy
Printer: Waterlow &
Sons Ltd
Registered: May 1899

Children's Plays and Pantomime

PLATE 51

Humpty Dumpty, or, Harlequin the Lost Princess and the Magic Silver Spoon

Theatre Royal, Exeter
20 December 1886

By Wilton Jones

This comic portrait of a flunkey advertised the first pantomime at the Theatre Royal, Exeter, leased and managed by Mr Sidney Herberte-Basing. Clare Harrington played the principal boy, Prince Prettyboy, while the title role was played by Fawcett Lomax whose clog dance 'secured for him the warmest encore of the evening' from a crowded first-night house.

One reviewer declared that Exeter had seen nothing better than 'this ingenious and fantastic pantomime' whose sets included 'the Magic Hen Coop', 'the Home of the Gnomes' and 'the Silver City'. The much-admired 'Porcelain' and 'Excelsior' ballets featured costumes designed by Wilhelm, a master of pantomime and ballet costume design.

The pantomime ended with an old-fashioned harlequinade, and included many coloured lighting effects, achieved by placing calico gauzes over the gas mantle cages. Less than a year later, in September 1887, a burning gauze was blamed as the cause of a disastrous fire at the theatre in which over two hundred 'galleryites' lost their lives.

PRO reference: COPY 1/76 folio 348
Artist: W H Pike
Printer: R W Stevens
Registered: December 1886

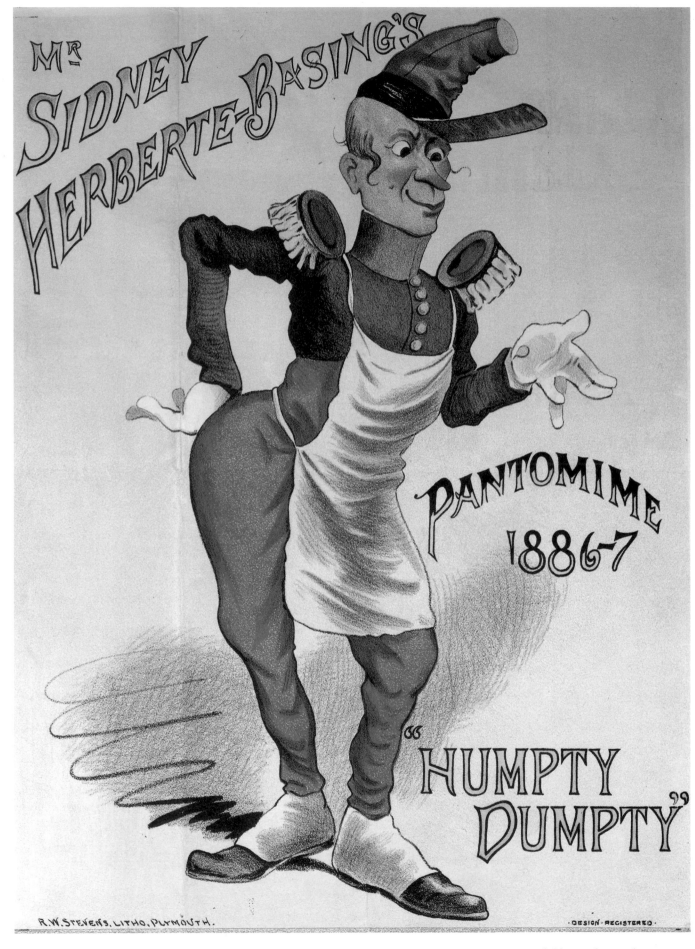

R.W. STEVENS. LITHO, PLYMOUTH.

·DESIGN·REGISTERED·

PLATE 52

Jack and the Beanstalk

Theatre Royal, Drury Lane,
26 December 1889

By Harry Nicholls
and Augustus Harris

Jack reveals a lot of leg in his scanty costume as he daintily climbs his beanstalk curiously composed of beanstalk fairies. This image aimed to entice audiences to Drury Lane Theatre for the eleventh annual pantomime mounted there by Augustus Harris – not that audiences needed much enticing since, by 1889, pantomimes at 'The Lane' were eagerly-awaited events, crammed full of spectacle, music, dancing and popular stars.

Pantomime needs a good Dame, and in this production Jack's mother, Mrs Simpson, was played by the best – the diminutive Dan Leno. The rotund Herbert Campbell was his perfect foil as Queen Fanny, the Flirt. Harriet Vernon was Jack, and the King of the Fairies was played by Agnes Hewitt, recovering no doubt from the bankruptcy she suffered that year as a result of her foray into theatrical management [see *The Golden Band*, plate 27]. Harry Nicholls, who played King Henry, was co-author with Augustus Harris.

Then, as now, pantomime thrived on topical references, so the depiction of the Eiffel Tower is not surprising. It was built in 1889 for the Paris Exposition and was much ridiculed for its 'absurd' construction.

PRO reference: COPY 1/88
folio 232
Artist: Charles Nicholson
Printer: Canning & Co.
Registered: December 1889

Children's Plays and Pantomime

PLATE 53

The Forty Thieves

Theatre Royal, Drury Lane,
26 December 1898

By Arthur Sturgess
and Arthur Collins

William True was dubbed 'the most versatile posterist of his day' in an interview published in *The Poster* magazine in July 1898. This striking image demonstrates his ingenuity as he incorporates the title into the design, the '40' flanking the image of the leggy 'thief' in her curiously tasselled costume.

This pantomime was another Drury Lane *tour de force*, but with Arthur Collins in control, who succeeded Augustus Harris in 1896. Collins was co-author of *Forty Thieves*, which starred Dan Leno as Abdalla, the Captain of the Thieves; Herbert Campbell in the Dame role as The Fair Zuleika; and Nellie Stewart as Drury Lane's first Australian principal boy. There were fourteen spectacular scenes designed by five scenic artists with locations as diverse as Khulja-a-sum-sum Street and Regent's Park Zoo. Act I featured a procession of 'The World's Collection of Porcelain', with 'the electrical effects of the Fairy Cascade'. The production was rounded off with a harlequinade starring the clown Whimsical Walker. It was a great success and ran until March 1899.

PRO reference: COPY 1/152
folio 108
Artist: Will. True
Printer: Waterlow & Sons Ltd
Registered: May 1899

Children's Plays and Pantomime

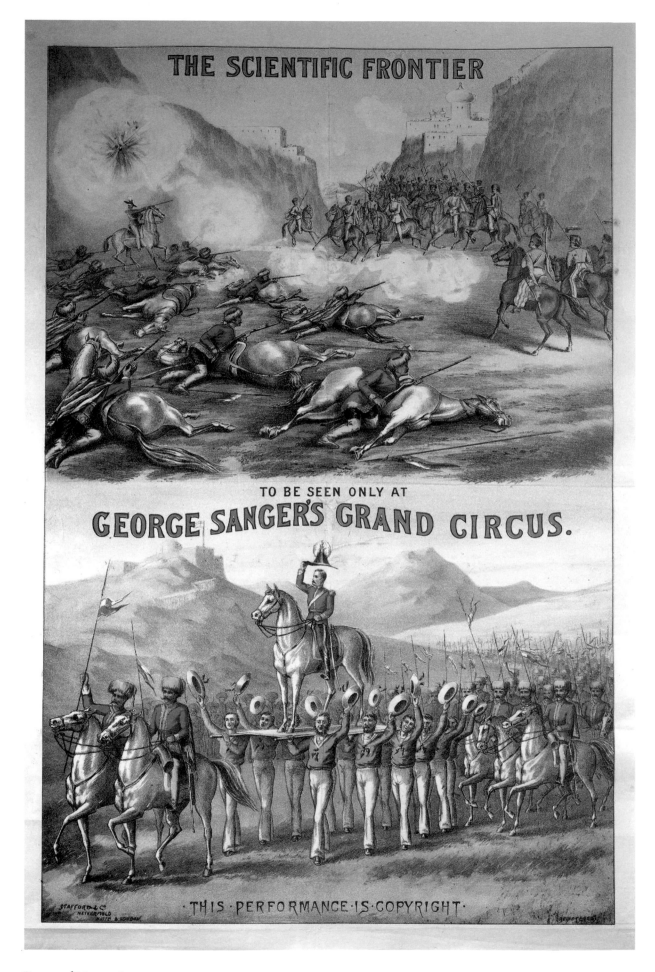

THE SCIENTIFIC FRONTIER

TO BE SEEN ONLY AT

GEORGE SANGER'S GRAND CIRCUS.

THIS · PERFORMANCE · IS · COPYRIGHT ·

PLATE 54

Sanger's Grand Circus

A modern viewer would not recognise this as a circus poster. There are no clowns or trapeze artists or even a hint of a circus ring, but a nineteenth-century circus-goer would immediately have recognised that it showed two scenes from an exciting horse drama re-enacted nightly at Sanger's Circus.

George Sanger, who styled himself 'Lord' George Sanger after 1887, was a great showman and perhaps the most successful 19th-century circus proprietor. From his early days in the 1850s, putting on conjuring shows and penny theatricals in fairground booths, he became the owner of a permanent circus building in London from 1871 to 1893, and built or owned circus buildings in at least ten other British towns. In 1899 he gave a command performance for Queen Victoria at Windsor Castle. He toured at home and on the continent with a circus that included as many as 160 horses, 11 elephants, 12 camels and 230 performers. The arrival of Sanger's circus in town was heralded by a spectacular parade.

PRO reference: COPY 1/79
folio 124
Artist: Thomas Phillips
Printer: Stafford & Co.
Registered: July 1887

Circus and Menagerie

PLATE 55

Hengler's Grand Cirque

'Equestrian wonders and novelties' were popular items on Victorian circus programmes. The artist of this poster ingeniously uses the three-dimensional letters of the word 'Cirque' as an obstacle over which this horse is jumping, complete with balancing jockey. The 'jockey act', in which equestrians dressed as jockeys vaulted on to galloping horses, was a well-known act in British circus by 1889, having been introduced by Andrew Ducrow in 1824.

Despite its name, Hengler's Cirque was a touring British circus owned by Frederick Charles Hengler and his brother, Albert Henry Hengler. Their father was a celebrated circus tightrope performer, and they had a tenting circus from about 1850. After 1860, Frederick and Albert preferred to present circus in permanent circus buildings: in Liverpool, Hull, Birmingham, Manchester, Bristol, Nottingham, Glasgow and Dublin. From 1887 to 1889, they ran Hengler's Circus in London, which was opened by their brother, Charles Hengler, in Argyll Street, where the London Palladium stands today. After 1889, they concentrated on their touring circus again; they had this poster designed and retained its copyright. The equestrian who performed the 'jockey act' in Hengler's Cirque at Birmingham in 1899 was Thomas Yelding.

PRO reference: COPY 1/86 folio 409
Artist: John Brown Thorp
Printer: none credited
Registered: April 1889

PLATE 56

PLATE 56

Edmond's (Late Wombwell's) Menagerie

A rather dismayed-looking lion is the centrepiece of this poster, and the Royal Crest above it appears almost as its tiara. The inclusion of an image of Queen Victoria was by no means inappropriate since she was a great lover of menagerie and circus. In 1830, the young Princess Victoria and her mother visited Wombwell's Menagerie at Thirsk, and there were command exhibitions of the menageries at Windsor Castle in 1834, 1842, 1847 and 1854.

Before the days of photography and television, the sight of strange live animals was a huge attraction. George Wombwell formed his first collection of animals in 1805, and by 1828 we know it was a lucrative business since it earned him £1,700 at Bartholomew Fair in 1828. He went on to create and run three menageries which toured Britain simultaneously. After his death, his no. 2 menagerie was run by his niece, Mrs Edmonds, until 1884, when she sold it to the Bostock family, the image of James Bostock featuring in the top right-hand roundel of this poster.

PRO reference: COPY 1/90
folio 385
Artist: Theophilus Creber
Printer: Creber Lith.
Registered: April 1890

Circus and Menagerie

PLATE 57

The Untamable Lion Wallace

Wallace was the fierce star of one of E H Bostock's travelling menageries. Born in 1858, Bostock was associated with the menagerie business from birth; his father, James Bostock, had become a menagerie owner after joining Edmonds' (late Wombwell's) Menagerie in 1839. As E H Bostock wrote: 'I was early accustomed to the laugh of the hyena, the roar of the lion, and the growl of the grizzly.'

Wallace was originally worked with three lionesses by E H Bostock's West Indian trainer, Sargano Alicamousa. After he left Bostock's menagerie in 1891, Bostock employed a new trainer, William Duncan, professionally known as 'Captain Rowley'. Rowley is depicted here in his act with Wallace. Despite his many daring bouts with Wallace in the 1890s, Rowley died peacefully in Glasgow in 1910, where he was buried in Lambhill Cemetery.

It is probably no coincidence that in Marriott Edgar's famous monologue, the lion who ate Albert was called Wallace.

PRO reference: COPY 1/109
folio 189
Artist: Theophilus Thomas Creber
Printer: Creber Lith.
Registered: August 1893

Circus and Menagerie

PLATE 58

Anderton and Haslam's United Shows and Menagerie

This poster for Anderton and Haslam's travelling menagerie features many of the animals that could be viewed, including a ferocious-looking bear and a wonderfully supercilious camel. The poster illustrates many of the feats that Captain Rowland performed in the menagerie cages, vying with similar acts that could be seen in circuses. Rowland later went into partnership with Anderton, and in 1928, Anderton and Rowland amalgamated their show with that of Madam Clara Paulo, continuing as Paulo's Circus.

Anderton and Haslam's poster announces that the entrance fee for 'all classes' was sixpence. In contrast, an advertisement of 1805 for Polito's Menagerie stated: 'Admittance (being Fair time) ladies and gentlemen one shilling – working people, servants and children, sixpence only'.

PRO reference:
COPY 1/114i
folio 20
Artist: Theophilus John Creber
Printer: Creber, Plymouth
Registered: July 1894

Circus and Menagerie

PLATE 59

Blondin's World's Fair

Royal Agricultural Hall, Islington

There was apparently no end to the variety of performance on offer to the patron of the 'World's Fair' at the Agricultural Hall, Islington, Christmas 1886. This poster shows vignettes of the circus, fairground and theatrical entertainment available, as well as a train steaming out of a prototype Channel tunnel, and the star attraction – the tightrope-walker, Blondin.

The Frenchman Jean François Gravelet – 'Blondin' – was sixty-two years old in 1886, but his reputation as the world's most daring tightrope walker meant that he was still in demand. In 1859 he crossed the Niagara Falls on a tightrope, turning a backwards somersault; by 1860 he was performing the stunt on stilts, blindfolded, sometimes pushing a wheelbarrow. When he appeared at the Crystal Palace in 1861, he was paid the then stupendous sum of £1,200 for twelve performances. He was

a consummate showman who agreed that a safety net was a sensible precaution – '*pour les autres*'. Even in retirement he took a daily walk along a tightrope set up in the garden of Niagara House, his home in Ealing.

PRO reference: COPY 1/76
folio 479
Artist: Theophilus Creber
Printer: Creber, Plymouth
Registered: 1886

PLATE 60

Rowe and Athol

This could certainly have been described as a 'novelty act' when it appeared on the variety stage. It appears to have been a 'Fishing Clown and Funny Frog' act, the part of the frog being taken by a contortionist who could perform on the trapeze and balance on chair backs. Rowe and Athol are shown here in roundels as serious young gentlemen, but this view of Rowe does little to redeem the ludicrous sight of him in his frog suit, complete with webbed feet, carrying his frog's head solemnly under his arm. He is described as 'the premier posturer of the world', and indeed, contortionists used to be called 'posture-masters' when they appeared as sideshows at fairs. Athol 'the elastic angler' was also an acrobat, who appeared as a white-faced clown, combining clowning with feats of balance with his froggy friend. There have probably been few acts like this since, which is hardly surprising.

PRO reference: COPY 1/69
folio 76
Artist: Dolph Levine
Printer: none credited
Registered: July 1885

PLATE 61

George Pike's Wonderful Performing Seals

The artist, Tom Merry, exploits the lovable, doe-eyed look of the seals to the utmost here. He positions their heads perfectly, so that the seals working the sewing machine and beating the drum seem intent on their pursuits, while three of the musician seals appear to be singing to their own accompaniment. Banjo-playing had been popularised by minstrel concerts in the 1880s, so George Pike was capitalising on a current craze by introducing this in his seals' act.

This troupe performed at variety theatres rather than circuses, as the inclusion of the theatrical curtains in the poster implies. Seals and sea-lions became popular circus acts, but they were introduced to the ring much later than other animals. The Englishman Captain Joseph Woodward is given the credit for first training seals in the 1880s, and his act was touring the halls at the same time as George Pike's. It was obviously important for Pike to have a good poster to advertise his act, and astutely, he retained the copyright of this.

PRO reference: COPY 1/78
folio 481
Artist: Tom Merry
Printer: Tom Merry Lith.
Registered: April 1887

TOM MERRY, DEL ET LITH, 102 & 104 NEWINGTON BUTTS, LONDON, S.E.

PLATE 62

Menotti the Stockholm Wonder High Telephone Wire Cyclist

Blondin was a tightrope-walking celebrity thirty years before Otto Menotti was performing, but this poster shows that Menotti reproduced some of Blondin's most famous feats with panache. Tom Merry's bird's eye view shows a city far below, with viewers nearer the action reeling back in amazement and throwing their hats into the air. The fact that Menotti is shown performing eight separate tightrope-walking feats at the same time does not seem to jar with the detailed realism of the city view.

The images of Menotti fill the space in the sky to great effect, so we suspend disbelief.

Blondin was still working in England in 1890 when Menotti was performing at the City Varieties Theatre in Leeds; *The Era*, 29 November 1890, carries advertisements for both. In June 1892, a case of breach of contract that Menotti brought against the proprietor of the Metropole Theatre, Birkenhead, shows he commanded £25 for a week's appearance. At London's Canterbury Music Hall, 19 August 1896, Menotti was the ninth act (following Dan Leno), and billed as 'The Stockholm

Wonder, King of the Telephone Wire'. 'The Stockholm Wonder' lived in Bootle when this poster was registered, and he was still touring British halls in 1906, advertising in the June issue of *The Performer* and giving his contact address as 51 Rockly Lane, Newsham Park, Liverpool.

PRO reference: COPY 1/85
folio 194
Artist: Tom Merry
Printer: Tom Merry Lith.; Menotti retained copyright
Registered: February 1889

PLATE 63

Morritt, the Leading Wonder Worker of the World

The magician Charles Morritt is shown here surrounded by various highlights of his act. In *The Variety Stage*, a book written in 1895 by Stuart and Park, Morritt was credited as one of the cleverest and most original illusionists of his day.

Born in Yorkshire in 1860, Morritt once owned the City of Varieties Theatre in Leeds. He came to London in 1859, and worked for four years with the famous magician Masklyne at the Egyptian Hall in London, leaving in 1893 to establish his own show at the Prince's Hall, also in Piccadilly. He was excellent at sleight-of-hand magic and 'telepathic' feats, both depicted here, but was most famous for his brilliantly staged cage illusion in which he produced people from an empty cage. For years Morritt also featured 'The Disappearing Donkey' in his act, the performing rights of which he sold to the escapologist Houdini.

PRO reference: COPY 1/107i folio 493
Artist: Arthur Benjamin Helsby
Printer: David Allen & Sons
Registered: December 1892

THE GREAT CONTINENTAL FACIAL KING

LORD·BEACONSFIELD·

·PRINCE·BISMARCK·

·WINDHORST·

·KING·OF·ITALY·

·EMP?·WILLIAM·II·

·QUEEN·VICTORIA·

·LISZT·

·LORD·BERESFORD·

·MOZART·

·GEN·GORDON·

·EMP?·WILLIAM·I·

·GEN·BOULANGER·

·HENRY·M·STANLEY·

·VICTOR·HUGO·

·EMP?·FREDRICK·III·

·EMP?·OF·AUSTRIA·

·DUKE·OF·WELLINGTON·

·H·R·H·PRINCE·OF·WALES·

·NAPOLEON·III·

·SHAH·OF·PERSIA·

·NAPOLEON·I·

·SHAKSPERE·

·GRAF·MOLTKE·

·R?·HON·W·E·GLADSTONE·

JOHN CRONOW IN HIS WONDERFUL ENTERTAINMENT 20 MINUTES AT MADAM TUSSAUDS

Variety

PLATE 64

The Great Continental Facial King John Cronow

This poster would not win any prizes for design, but it served its purpose, depicting famous personalities whose features 'facial king' Cronow imitated. His peculiar talent seems to have been as a quick-change make-up artist with wigs, sideburns, hats and headdresses adopted and discarded at speed, to change him from Queen Victoria to her son, the Prince of Wales, and then to Shakespeare. The title of his act – 'Twenty Minutes at Madame Tussaud's' – reflects the contemporary popularity of the wax-work exhibition, as well as Cronow's comparison of his creations to live waxworks.

Cronow's own face is depicted in a roundel suspended on ribbon, as if his were the face on a prize-winning medal. Without undue modesty, he described himself as 'The Great Continental Facial King'. From his billing as 'Herr Cronow, Imperial Facialist' at the Canterbury Music Hall, 31 October 1898, it seems that he was German. He appeared that night with well-known English top-liners, including Marie Lloyd and George Robey.

PRO reference: COPY 1/93 folio 196
Artist: Halbert
Printer: none credited; Cronow retained copyright
Registered: December 1890

PLATE 65

Arthur Strode

Arthur Strode does not seem like
a name to conjure with but he
obviously did, successfully
enough to commission his own
poster. Including a skull, a
serpent, owls, toads and an
incense burner in his poster, the
artist attempted to convey the
supernatural atmosphere of
Strode's act. The levitating lady
floats eerily in a starlit sky, but
combined with a sombre portrait
of Strode in a decorated roundel,
busy lettering and a riverside
setting, the result is more manic
than magic. Nevertheless, it
shows that Strode aimed to
weave his tricks into a dramatic
presentation, despite his rather
formal evening dress!

Strode may well have been
influenced by the American
magician Charles Andress, who
toured North America for over
fifty years with his show.
Curiously, one of Andress's
posters featured silhouettes of
devils with pitchforks around an
incense burner, a levitating lady
and the words 'Magic, Mirth and
Mystery' – strikingly similar to
the description of Strode's act as
'Mirth, Magic and Mystery'. In
England, Strode's more successful
contemporary magicians included
Charles Morritt [see plate 63] and
the favourite magician of the
Prince of Wales, Charles Bertram,
who asked his audience after
every trick, 'Isn't it wonderful?'

PRO reference: COPY 1/106i
folio 185
Artist: Dominic Hand
Printer: Dominic Hand's Sons,
London
Registered: September 1892

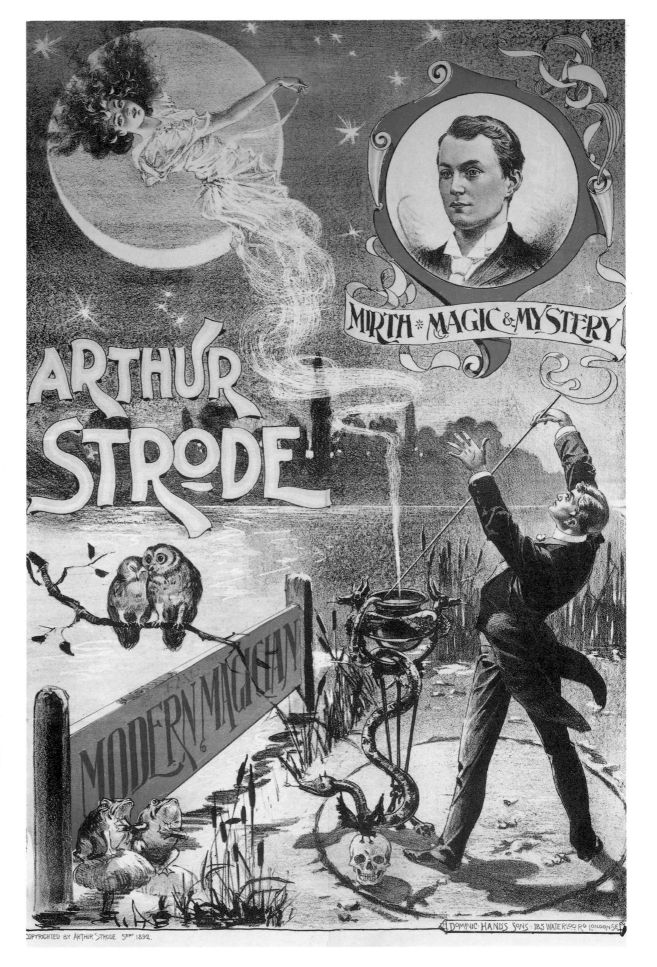

PLATE 66

The Beautiful Florences

In December 1890, Ani Florence and Ino Charles – 'The Beautiful Florences' – advertised their act, in *The Era*, as:

> 'Unanimously praised. The World's Daring Mid-Air Beauties … the amazing Aerial Puzzlers, in their novel and mysterious Performance on the Frame of Life. Success not to be equalled.'

Like the poster for Menotti's aerial act [see plate 62], the artist depicts his subjects performing in the open air. The rays of the setting sun radiate upwards into the sky; a star shines down from behind the lettering announcing the name of this act. The central image shows the girls performing their 'teeth-spinning' act, with the colours of their costumes reflected in the green, yellow and red colouring of the word 'Florences'. The girls' faces appear in roundels, while highlights of their act, including work on the flying trapeze, are shown in the sky around them and in decorative frames below.

'Aerial athletes' was the term applied in the 19th century to all aerial performers such as the Florences and Gertrella [see plate 67]. A 'dental athlete' was one who could perform the feat of spinning in mid-air, suspended from a revolving metal hook attached to a leather strap held between the teeth. Teeth marks on surviving leather straps used by performers of this act bear witness to the strength of their incisors and the force with which the strap had to be clenched between the teeth.

PRO reference: COPY 1/115i folio 204
Artist: Robert Daniel Livado
Printer: Averys Ltd
Registered: October 1894

PLATE 67

Graceful Gertrella

Gertrella was clearly an accomplished aerial performer, and one whose minimal costume showed off her wasp waist to good advantage. The vigour and detail of this design shows that the artist relished his subject, depicting as many moments as possible from her act. A sky-effect background around the central figure of Gertrella gives a sense of height, while a feeling of movement is achieved by the depiction of the ribbons on her costume flying in the air.

Aerial performers were popular items on the bill in late Victorian and Edwardian variety theatres, where they often performed over the auditorium, as shown in the lower left-hand part of the poster. Gertrella is shown doing a fashionable 'skirt dance' on the tightrope, but the most spectacular part of her performance was on the flying trapeze, an act which had proven immensely popular after the French aerialist Leotard invented it in 1859. Gertrella had this poster designed and registered in 1895; she was still performing in May 1903, when she was paid £18 by Moss Empire Ltd for a week's appearances at the Holloway Empire.

PRO reference: COPY 1/117 folio 101
Artist: Charles Frederick Noble
Printer: David Allen
Registered: March 1895

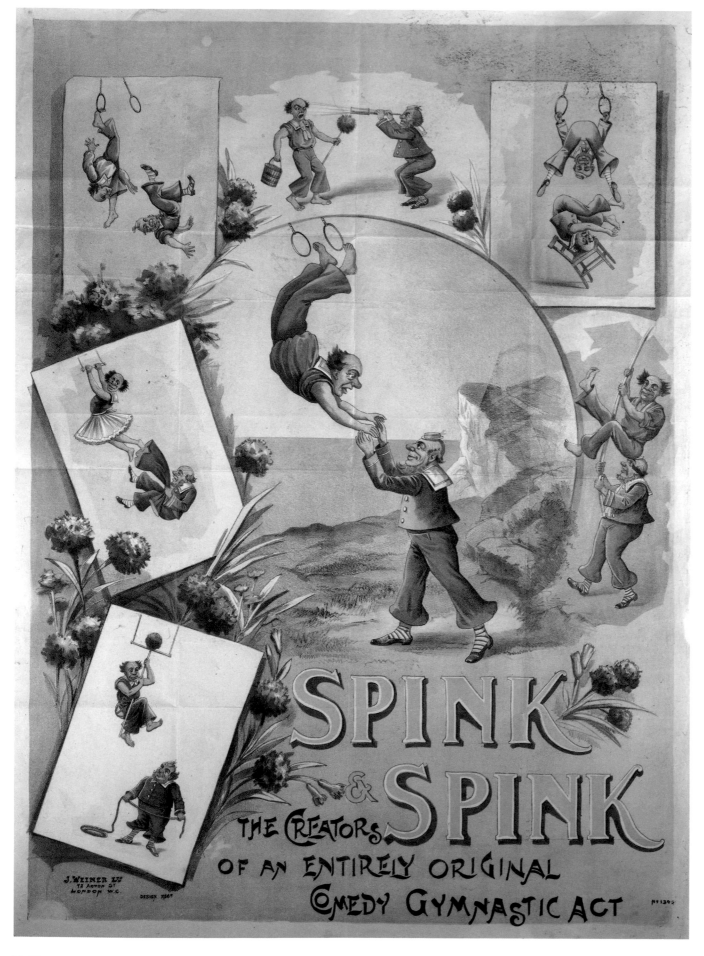

PLATE 68

Spink & Spink

Spink & Spink describe themselves here as 'the creators of an entirely original comedy gymnastic act', and in their advertisement in *The Era*, 17 November 1894, they called themselves 'Nautical Gymnastic Drolls' and their act a 'Comedy Gymnastic Absurdity', noting that they were 'knocking lumps off them at the Argyle, Birkenhead'! The following week they were at the Palace, Nottingham, and after that at the Empire, Hull. When they appeared at Barnard's Palace of Varieties, Chatham during the week beginning 8 December – on the same bill as a comedian, a singer, a comedy sketch and a short play – a reviewer wrote briefly: 'Spink & Spink are a decided success.'

The flowers and the cliff view appear to be the artist's flight of fancy, although the sea view relates to the nautical flavour of their act. The poster shows their sailor costumes as well as the pink skirt that one of them wore at one point in the act. They were obviously accomplished gymnasts as well as talented clowns, since good timing is just as essential for apparent failure at catches as it is for success.

PRO reference: COPY 1/123 folio 189
Artist: Chadwyck Rymer
Printer: Weiner's Ltd
Registered: December 1895

PLATE 69

R A Roberts, the Protean Actor

'Protean actors' needed the skills of quick-change artists, impressionists and actors. In the late 19th century they were a popular act on the variety stage, grandly dubbed 'Protean' after the Greek god Proteus, who could change his shape at will. One theatre-goer writing in 1916 recalled 'an outbreak of so-called "Protean" art in the London music halls. I believe its exponents were extremely well-paid.'

R A Roberts was one of the most well known 'protean actors' of the turn of the century. Born in Liverpool in 1870, he began his career there, performing on stage after working as a merchant's clerk. He appeared at the Rotunda Theatre, Liverpool, in 1885, and then with various companies, including that of Andrew Melville. After three years at London's Egyptian Hall with Maskelyne and Cook, he performed at music halls, including the Palace Theatre, London, in 1899, and the Holloway Empire in 1903, where he received the generous sum of over £27 a week. By 1909, when Roberts appeared at the Oxford Music Hall, he was earning £55 a week; Wilkie Baird received £60, and Marie Lloyd got £80, but others on the same bill received between £6 and £18 a week.

Dick Turpin, depicted here, was one of his favourite characters, which he performed successfully in 1905 in London and New York. Another of his favourites was Mrs Twiddles in *Lucinda's Experiment*, a character less commonly recognised today.

PRO reference: COPY 1/220i folio 422
Artist: Arthur Brooke White
Printer: David Allen & Sons
Registered: September 1904

PLATE 70

The Beautiful Mademoiselle Nadji

Arthur Penniall clearly revelled in the task of designing this poster, and created a busy but extremely attractive image which shows the range of this act and the charms of its exponent. Mademoiselle Nadji appears to have been principally a contortionist who specialised in back-bending, but from the view of her suspended below the platform, we see that she included a dash of teeth-spinning for good measure.

The poster shows a head-and-shoulders portrait of the respectably hatted Mademoiselle Nadji, and an image of her demurely sitting in a stage box. Having thus established that she could be the girl next door, Penniall shows her full-length in a provocative pose, dressed in her revealing blue costume with gold-tasselled sash and white tights. Her silver staircase was illuminated by electric bulbs, a novelty which hints at lavish pantomime 'walk-downs'. Since she performed in music halls all over the country, the staircase would have been a cumbersome prop to transport.

PRO reference:
COPY 1/222
folio 144
Artist: Arthur Penniall
Printer: Oldfield & Co.
Registered: October 1904

PLATE 71

**Grais' Zebras
and Baboons**

This was another act which would have appeared on stage at variety theatres in England before the First World War. Circuses were faring badly by 1911, when this poster was registered, and many 19th-century permanent circus buildings had been closed. Even elephant acts were featured in variety.

Zebras had been seen in circuses as early as 1780, when Philip Astley led one around his circus ring. In 1832 Andrew Ducrow featured four zebras in his circus in a 'wild zebra hunt', which he illustrated on an advertisement, their elegant stripes making them ideal subjects for an engraving. Monkeys on horseback, an act known even in Elizabethan days, was also featured in 19th-century circus. Baboons were trained as jockeys of horses and donkeys in the circus later in the century. Even if Grais's act was not especially innovative in 1911, this poster was designed to make it seem spectacular and amusing at a time when nobody questioned the ethics of watching animals performing.

PRO reference: COPY 1/315i
folio 38
Artist: Albert Whitfield
Printer: Moody Bros, Birmingham
Registered: November 1911

PLATE 72

Marvelle

When Marvelle's dogs were performing at London's Empire Theatre in June 1892, the following advertisement appeared in *The Era:*

> 'Marvelle. Emperor of the Canine world, with the only Dog Circus on Earth. The Smartest and Best Show on the Road. The Largest Performing Boarhounds ever seen on any Stage, not forgetting the original dog, Rags.'

Rags is depicted in the central roundel of this poster, executing one of his champion somersaults, surrounded by images of other highlights of the act. The German Boarhound does not exist as a breed nowadays, but it was similar to the Great Dane, although not as tall or long in the body.

There appears to have been some rivalry between Marvelle's 'canine wonders' and Parker's American Dogs who, the same month, were appearing at the Gaiety Palace, Birmingham. A week after Marvelle's advertisement, Parker advertised his act as 'the Best Dog Circus on Earth', noting pointedly: 'I am the originator of the Smart working Dog Circus. Notice – the first dog ever taught to do a back somersault is by name "Jack" and belongs to Mr Watson (in America), late of P T Barnum's Circus.'

PRO reference: COPY 1/91
folio 189
Artist: Henry Abdy
Printer: Stafford & Co.
Registered: September 1901

PLATE 73

Tom Cannon

The Lancastrian Tom Cannon was hardly 'the Champion Wrestler of the World' – he wasn't even the British champion, but he was a regional wrestling champion in the Liverpool area in the 1890s. By 1895, when this poster was registered, he had joined the variety hall circuit to show his wrestling prowess as an act. He wrestled with another professional on stage, as can be seen from the roundels on this poster, illustrating different holds and throws. He would probably also have challenged a spectator to wrestle with him, although the one he chose may well have been another professional deliberately planted in the audience.

It is not surprising that wrestling took to the variety stage since it has always displayed ample scope for theatricality. Cannon's more famous contemporary Lancastrian wrestler, Connors, went by the name of 'Little Pompey', but it appears that Cannon had no such sobriquet. The showmanship of wrestling was demonstrated to a much wider audience in the 1960s, when the sport was televised.

PRO reference: COPY 1/117
folio 97
Artist: James Affleck
Printer: David Allen & Sons
Registered: February 1895

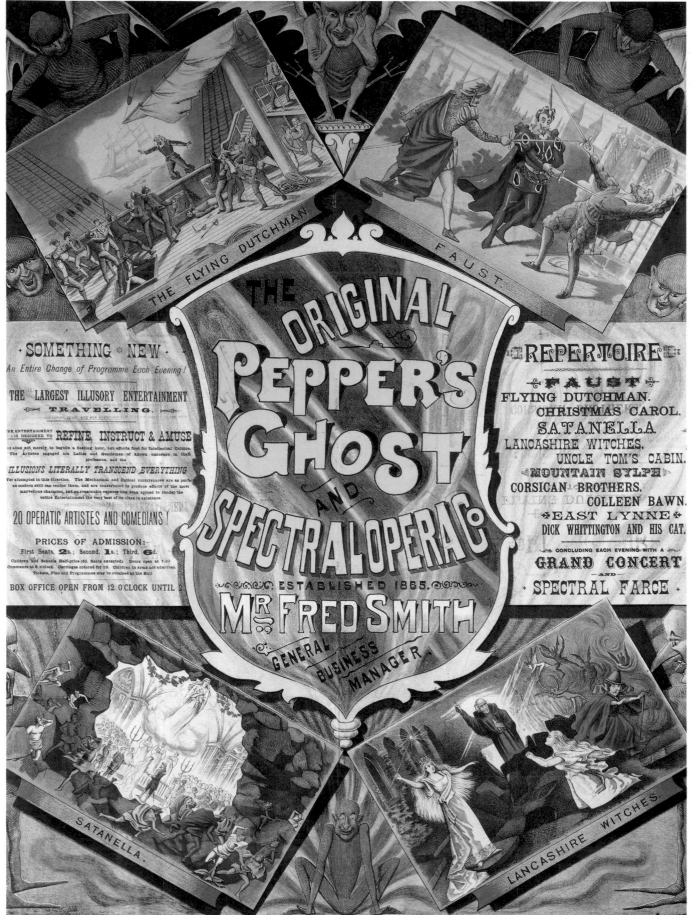

PLATE 74

The Original Pepper's Ghost and Spectral Opera Company

With winged, grotesque creatures leering down, this poster conjures images from four of the operatic and dramatic productions featured on tour by this company. The common theme was the supernatural – the ghosts in *A Christmas Carol* and *The Corsican Brothers*. Frederick and Emily Smith specialised in creating stage apparitions by a technique known as 'Pepper's Ghost', after Professor Pepper, who first exhibited the phenomenon in 1863. An optical effect produced an image behind a sheet of glass when lit from the front. If a large sheet of glass was placed beneath the stage at a certain angle, with actors concealed from the audience there, lighting could project their ghostly images on to the stage.

The Smiths formed their company in 1869 and toured with performances of 'short opera music, designed pictures and spectral illusions'. They often appeared in Ireland, and were so successful that, in 1891, a rival company advertised in Londonderry with the same name. In December 1892, the Smiths were granted an injunction against their competitor. This poster reaffirmed the Smiths' as: 'The *Original* Pepper's Ghost and Spectral Opera Company'.

PRO reference: COPY 1/108i folio 276
Artist: James Fitzpatrick
Printer: The Irish Printing and Bookbinding Works Ltd
Registered: June 1893

Minstrels and Spectacles

The ORIENT OLYMPIA'S Grandest Show ON EARTH
in London

terranean Hall of 1001 Columns   TWICE DAILY   Thousands of 1ˢᵗ Reserved SEATS Including Admission

PLATE 75

The Orient
Olympia, December 1894

The late 19th-century taste for theatrical spectacle knew no bounds, and the men who knew how to satisfy it in London were two Hungarian brothers, Imre and Bolossy Kiralfy. This poster advertises *The Orient*, a combination of lavish theatrical spectacle and 'oriental experience' produced by Bolossy Kiralfy at Olympia from December 1894 until July 1895.

This subterranean waterway was originally created for *Venice in London* –

Imre Kiralfy's mammoth production which had opened at Olympia in 1891. The plaster columns were built over wire netting frames, and during *Venice in London*, visitors could take gondola tours on the 'canals'. When *Venice* finished, Bolossy Kiralfy was invited to produce an equally ambitious spectacle – *Constantinople* – which opened in December 1893 and retained the Venetian canal, re-vamped as the waterways of Constantinople. This was kept for the 'grand aquatic pageant' in *The Orient*, Bolossy's next production which opened only a month after the

closure of *Constantinople*, in November 1894. *The Orient* featured over 2,500 performers, and the opening-day attendance of 34,537 broke all records for Olympia, initially justifying its massive publicity campaign. Audiences dropped drastically during the winter however, and *The Orient* was forced to close in July 1895.

PRO reference: COPY 1/116
folio 205
Artist: Alfred Rava
Printer: none credited
Registered: January 1895

Minstrels and Spectacles

EMPIRE OF INDIA EXHIBITION

1895

DIRECTOR GENERAL

IMRE KIRALFY

EARL's COURT

Admission 1/-
Season Ticket 10/6

COPYRIGHTED 1895 BY THE LONDON EXHIBITIONS LIMITED.

PRINTED IN PARIS BY LEMERCIER

PLATE 76

Empire of India Exhibition

Earl's Court, May 1895

Before British people could easily travel abroad, Imre and Bolossy Kiralfy transported 'abroad' to London, with spectacular success. Imre Kiralfy had mounted Venice in Olympia in 1894; his brother Bolossy recreated Constantinople there in 1893, and aspects of the Orient there later that year [see plate 75]. On 27 May 1895, Imre Kiralfy's *Empire of India Exhibition* opened at Earl's Court. Complete with jungle, an Indian city and music from the bands of the Grenadier and Coldstream Guards, it was 'a living picture of India', according to the *Illustrated London News*.

The programme for the exhibition (price, one penny) listed performances which took place in various areas. In the Burmese Palace, 'genuine Burmese Girls and Boys clad in typical national costume' exhibited their dances every half-hour, from 2 p.m. until 10.30 p.m. There was a display of Burmese wrestling, and 'Genuine Burmese Cheroots, rolled by Girls from Moulmein' were available at the stall outside the palace, 'at popular prices'. There was a menagerie, an Electrophone providing listening facilities to various London theatres, as well as the fairground attractions, the 'Switchback' and 'The Gigantic Wheel'. Imre repeated his success the following year with an *Empire of India and Ceylon Exhibition*, and in 1901 brought a *Chinese Military Spectacle* to Earl's Court, followed by *Paris in London*, 1902.

PRO reference: COPY 1/118i
folio 228
Artist: Louis Marold
Printer: none credited
Registered: May 1895

PLATE 77

Miss Lucy Moore

Lucy Moore turned her weight to her advantage and made a career out of being exhibited as 'The Heaviest Female in the World'. Exaggerated claims like this were often made for personalities and performers before the days of the Advertising Standards Authority.

Long before theatres were established in Europe, fairs provided showgrounds for acrobats, magicians, actors, musicians, performing animals, puppeteers and showmen exhibiting the latest 'Freak of Nature'. The 'freaks' included so-called giants, Siamese twins, and even people who looked different simply because they came from another country. Before the days of illustrated publications, television and film, people had little idea about the world, and limited experience outside their own communities.

At London's Bartholomew Fair in 1828 there is evidence of the lucrative takings for similar sideshows: 'exhibition of pig-faced lady, £130; ditto, fat boy and girl, £140; the Chinese jugglers, £50; exhibition of a Scottish giant, £20'. Bertram Mills's first circus at Olympia featured sideshows, and as late as the 1920s, Mills proudly advertised the exhibition of 'The Ring-Necked Women from Upper Burma'.

PRO reference: COPY 1/223ii folio 249
Artist: Edward Thomas Day Stevens
Printer: Willsons' Printers
Registered: October 1904

PLATE 78

Moore and Burgess Minstrels

'Fun without vulgarity' – this minstrel troupe prided themselves on the propriety of their shows. Many types of public entertainment were still regarded with distaste by the gentility when Moore and Burgess originally collaborated in 1870, but with their shows at the St James's Hall in London's Piccadilly, the Moore and Burgess Minstrels wooed and won the respectable classes. They finally disbanded thirty years

later, in 1900, after a final performance at St Leonard's Pier Pavilion, one commentator describing theirs as 'a show that had never lent itself to questionable dialogue or double entendre'.

The American minstrel comedian George Washington Moore first appeared in England at St James's Hall in 1859, with Raynor and Pierce's Christy Troupe. Moore started his own Christy troupe in 1864, but his real success began when he went into

partnership with his business manager, Frederick Burgess. Burgess was an astute publicist and would have approved this poster proudly depicting the full complement of the troupe.

PRO reference: COPY 1/123
folio 200
Artist: Chadwick Rymer
Printer: Weiner's Ltd
Registered: December 1895

Minstrels and Spectacles

PLATE 79

Lieutenant Morgan's Water Show

This poster makes even the most overcrowded melodrama poster seem restrained. 'The King of the Waves' peppered his poster with images of incidents from his show – labelling them, should the viewer be in doubt. 'The Ladies' Cycle Races' appear entertaining, but not as much as the 'Battle of the Bladders' or 'Cricket on the Surface of the Water'!

Water shows were not uncommon in the late 19th century, either at Earl's Court or Olympia, or at theatres which could adapt their stages to be flooded for the purpose. London even boasted the Westminster Aquarium and Summer and Winter Garden, where exhibitions of swimming and diving regularly took place. Lieutenant Morgan's show appears to have originated in America, but Captain Boyton's water show was Britain's home-grown example of the species.

PRO reference: COPY 1/152 folio 104
Artist: Lieutenant L Morgan
Printer: Waterlow & Sons Ltd
Registered: May 1899

PLATE 80

Buffalo Bill's Wild West

The imposing figure of Buffalo Bill is bathed in the light of the blaze behind him as he shades his eyes and scans the horizon. The lettering of the words 'Wild West' is licked by flame, but our hero is seen here as invincible – the star of the show.

William Frederick Cody, born in Iowa in 1846, became Colonel Cody and the showman Buffalo Bill. He spent the first half of his life living dramatic episodes in America's Wild West, and the second half recreating them in epic shows across America and England. Cody really did drive the Deadwood Coach from Cheyenne and Deadwood; he shot buffalo, survived Red Indian attacks and knew the sharp-shooting Annie Oakley. Even Queen Victoria came to see his Wild West Show at Earl's Court in 1887 – and this during the years of her self-imposed ban on theatre-going in reverence to the memory of her late Consort, Prince Albert. Cody was still performing successfully fifteen years later and this poster was produced for a two-year tour of Great Britain that he embarked on in 1903. That followed a season at Olympia which opened in December 1902 and received another royal visit early in 1903, this time from the King and Queen with a clutch of royal children.

PRO reference: COPY 1/210i folio 301
Artist: Alick Penrose Ritchie
Printer: Weiner's Ltd
Registered: October 1903

Minstrels and Spectacles